ISBN-13: 9798727238400
ISBN-10: 1477123456

Cover design by: Art Painter
Library of Congress Control Number: 2018675309
Printed in the United States of America

I0481017

CONTENTS

LESSONS

From

The Great Recession - 2008...

Mistrust Dishonesty

&

Justice Dismissed

A BURSTING INTEGRITY BUBBLE

1. LESSONS - INTRODUCTION

In 2019, I was coping with the shocking and consequential confrontations of the prior decade, especially the final three years. I had to focus and find a way to explain to a loyal financial partner and my stressed-out family how things happened. While I rummaged through hundreds of pages of legal documents, depositions, memoranda, and numerous digital files on my computer, I sought to construct an honest and concise report for all. Then I read an article in the New York Times.

Robert J. Shiller, the Nobel Laureate economist, wrote in the New York Times on November 8, 2019: "How Lying and Mistrust Could Hurt the American Economy." In it he says: "An atmosphere generated by a steady flow and variety of lies is like a dark cloud over the facts. Businesses cannot plan effectively when they don't know who or what can be trusted. At the moment, we don't know the extent to which lying, and mistrust have already permeated the entire culture."

Few American economic sectors are more vulnerable to lying and mistrust than small businesses and their essential personal interactions. I have a well-documented story. My 25-year office services business and I unexpectedly drove into that dark cloud of lying and mistrust, even as the popular business was thriving in the rapidly expanding shared-workspace, coworking, flex-space industry. I cannot know the full economic extent of these behavioral patterns. However, I do know the financial and reputational damage and pain they created for me, and my small business in Greenwich, CT. during the Great Recession, and its consequential aftermath. This is my story.

2. LESSONS – AUTHOR

Frank B. McBrearity, Jr.

Frank McBrearity was the Managing Member and Chief Executive of CEO Holly Hill, LLC, the owner of Corporate Executive Offices (CEO), an executive suite, shared offices and co-working business in Greenwich, CT. CEO was a favored home to more than 100 businesses including: investors, investment advisors, hedge funds, public relations and advertising firms, attorneys, executive search, and a variety of other entrepreneurial enterprises. Many firms enjoyed "virtual" status with a prominent business address and access to conference rooms, networking spaces and support services. CEO was founded in 1988 and had a long-standing presence in the Greenwich office services sector. McBrearity and partners acquired the business in late 2003.

From 1993 to 2004, McBrearity was President & CEO of McBrearity & Co., Inc. In that period, the firm was a partner and the sole agent, advisor, and asset manager to the IBUS Companies, a Dutch investment organization, regarding their U.S. investment program. Over the 1993 to 2001 period, McBrearity oversaw the acquisition, financing, asset management and disposition of IBUS' $300 million U.S. portfolio, including repositioning, lease-up, new construction, accounting, and financial reporting. The portfolio included office, retail, and multifamily investments, in ten metropolitan markets, including major office properties in Boston, Washington, DC, Minneapolis, Indianapolis, Charlotte and Richmond. The portfolio's assets were sold between 1999 and 2002. McBrearity was a VP and Director of IBUS USA, Inc. over that period.

3

Prior to his own company, McBrearity was President of Baring Institutional Realty Advisors, Landauer Advisors and a Managing Director of Landauer Associates, Inc. a national real estate consultant. Investor/clients included Citic Investments, Inc. (Holland and Belgium), British Shell Petroleum Co., Yasuda Life Insurance, Fuji Bank, and the pension funds of CalPers, Honeywell and GenCorp.

McBrearity is a graduate of Villanova University and the University of Chicago Graduate School of Business. In his early career, he was active in the Urban Land Institute and the American Society of Real Estate Counselors. He was a resident of New Canaan, CT since 1984 where he was Treasurer, Vice Chairman and Director of the United Way of New Canaan, Inc., and a Director on the Board of The Norwalk Emergency Shelter, Inc. (now, The Open Door). After acquiring CEO, McBrearity became active on the Board of the Greenwich Chamber of Commerce, becoming Corporate Secretary in 2014 and Chairman in 2017.

3. LESSONS - PROLOGUE

October 2008 - The Housing Bubble

As I drove to my Greenwich, CT business that October morning, I was still celebrating my daughter's wedding to her British fiancé the prior weekend. It was a joyful celebration with family members from both countries, plus many high-school and college friends from the area. The autumn weather was perfect; sunny and mild, offering pleasant outdoor experiences for the British visitors. The reception venue overlooking Stamford harbor was festive and photogenic. A British-style band introduced us to Coldplay throughout the evening.

Without thinking, I turned on the car radio. It was not music now. The business news of the prior two weeks reverberated: stock market declines at record levels, an Emergency Stabilization Act in preparation, anxiety at the International Monetary Fund, and talk of a "systemic meltdown." Rescue plans were surfacing. The bursting "housing bubble" of last year had serious, widespread implications.

I turned off the radio and refocused on the area's transformation over the 20th century in response to a unique coastline, picturesque countryside, rail transit service and Interstate highways. Greenwich had become a gateway for corporations, financial firms, and other organizations seeking modern and economical satellite installations, with lower tax rates. In time, such names as General Electric, United Technologies and Xerox lined the major highways.

Many leading executives chose to reside in Greenwich as it evolved from a special enclave for the wealthy, in the early years, into a thriving business and residential destination embracing affluent households with strong ties to the economy. Somewhat known for bankers, philanthropists, and entertainment notables, it had become a home for the financially secure, largely insulated from economic turmoil. I wondered, "What could they be thinking now?" as the morning commuter traffic was minimal. When I entered downtown the nearby parking lots were almost empty and the Town's commercial center, unusually quiet.

I arrived rather early at Two Sound View Drive, the headquarters of my 20-year executive office suite/business center, Corporate Executive Offices (CEO), with more than 60 office clients in occupancy. Staff had not yet come in and few clients were evident in their offices.

As I entered our coffee bar adjoining the reception area, I saw a long-term CEO client who looked bewildered and ashen as he stared at the coffee machine. He had been a partner with Goldman Sachs, widely regarded for his extensive experience with multi-national industrial corporations. He was retired from Goldman but remained in an emeritus role to facilitate continuity with these long- term relationships. He often arrived early for private calls with his European contacts. This morning was no exception.

When he caught my eye again, he said: "I have just been on the phone with BASF in Germany for the past couple of hours. They have been a client of mine through Goldman for years. What I learned this morning is terrifying. They told me that on Tuesday and Wednesday this week BASF did not have an order for anything, anywhere in the world -- for two whole days, no inquiries, no phones ringing, or computers flashing. Their business world was silent and is still incredibly quiet. They confirmed this with others. The firm has been in business for more than 100 years and never witnessed this experience. Everything has stopped."

As I walked around, the CEO business was unusually subdued. Many rented offices were dark as clients were absent. No meetings or visitors were evident. Few phone calls rang at reception. The atmosphere was in stark contrast to the prior weekend in New Canaan. Now it appeared something was seriously amiss.

A couple days later, a regional executive with Wells Fargo Bank, who had a corner office at CEO, sat motionless in the conference room staring out the window. Mary Bennett, our receptionist, had alerted me earlier, "He's been sitting there sullen and rather inactive for a couple of days. Things are unusually quiet, so I haven't bothered."

I approached to reach out. "Oh hi," he said. "Sorry if I'm creating a problem. I have been on the phone with my clients here in Greenwich, and with senior executives in New York and San Francisco. Feedback is grim. I want away from my phone." He shook his head and looked out the windows again. After a long pause he looked back and said, "No one in our generation will ever forget the day Lehman Brothers went bankrupt! It's our financial 9/11 on September 15, 2008."

The comment resurrected horrifying memories of that quiet Tuesday morning in New Canaan. It was 8:45 and my son called from his office in White Plains. "Dad, what's going on? I am sitting here seeing this huge plume of smoke rising from lower Manhattan. What happened?"

I quickly turned on the television and watched the terrorist attack unfold in real time. Soon the phone rang again. My daughter was calling from Atlanta asking: "Dad, where's Brad? Everyone is calling me about him. He works in the World Trade Center." Brad was a special friend from high school and college years. He was on the 89th floor of the South Tower. His parents were neighbors and good friends.

Is this the new reality seven years later? Are the consequences of 9/15/08 likely to be as traumatizing as those of 9/11/01? I could not set that thought aside as I walked the corridors of Corporate

Executive Offices that day.

On the following Monday, CEO staff discovered a client sound asleep under the large conference room table at 8:00 in the morning. The first arrivals were shocked, thinking he was unconscious. Staff soon assisted him to his office where they discovered he had already deployed a sleeping bag. They had earlier advised, "Mr. Fitz was not leaving the office at the end of the day. He is not taking calls from wife or family. Everything goes to voicemail."

We all knew he had been an investment adviser and a senior partner with a very prominent investment management firm in New York City. The firm was acquired by Lehman Brothers in 2003, and Mr. Fitz became the beneficiary of a significant shareholding in Lehman. Sometime after the merger he retired and, in 2006, relocated his files to his new Greenwich office at CEO, where he offered investment advice to a small clientele and managed his own portfolio. In that year, he had purchased an oceanfront tract on Nantucket Island and soon initiated development of a waterfront estate, apparently with financing secured by his Lehman shares. Now as we approached the end of October, his family and friends came to check the situation, close his CEO account, and expedite the removal of his files, computer, fax machine and personal items. Mr. Fitz was moving home.

These events and interactions in the office exemplified the stress and anxiety already evident throughout the Greenwich business environment. Everyone was aware that the parking lots near the Metro North commuter station, usually full by 6:00 or 6:30 in the morning, now remained vacant.

My staff asked repeatedly, "Frank, what is happening? We have no meetings. We have little phone activity, many new clients, but few are ever in their offices."

Mary often asked, "Where is Pat Ashton? Have you heard from him, or his brother? It has been quite a while since either has been in the office. There are lots of messages in their voicemails."

I had not heard anything from Pat or his colleagues. Bill Day was the only client who seemed to be in his office every day, often helping his son with his senior year high school activities in the small conference room.

Pat and I had met in the early 1980's when he was with Lehman Brothers exploring real estate ventures that Lehman might finance in Southeast Florida. He retained my firm, Landauer Associates, in West Palm Beach to evaluate opportunities and relationships. It was twenty-five years later, and he had become a client again.

I soon walked back to his office at the far end of the suite. It was a larger room often occupied by two or three. I unlocked the door, switched on the lights, and saw a once active office with computers, documents, and files arrayed on the desks. The message lights were flashing on all the telephones.

As I looked in, I noticed some eye-catching artifacts on the walls and bookcases exposing an extensive collection of New York baseball memorabilia. Framed photographs and illustrations were everywhere, each autographed by an All-Star from a prior era: Joe DiMaggio, Yogi Berra, Casey Stengel, Roy Campanella, Whitey Ford, Mickey Mantle, Roger Maris, and many others. The office had been left unattended. Several months of rent were due.

I returned to the front desk. "Mary, I locked Pat's office door. Please tell Terri and Donna that no one is permitted in that office, including the cleaning crew, until further word from me. Put a sign on the door 'Do not enter'."

After a pause, I added: "This is our twentieth year of business. An anniversary celebration is scheduled for the December holiday party. We should make sure it is a great time for all. We'll salute Bill Day, Robin Davis, and other clients from the beginning."

I quietly returned to my office and reflected on my business career, searching for anything comparable to these circumstances. The Vietnam War, and its repercussions, were in the background through graduate school in Chicago. The Savings & Loan Crisis of the late 1980s preceded the recession of the early 1990s. Then the dot.com bubble. Yet nothing approached what I was witnessing now in Greenwich. Could this really be a 9/11 type of event, on 9/15/2008? I sat down with the realization that this could continue to resonate for quite some time.

4. LESSONS - PRELUDE

2003 - The Dot.Com Bubble

It was late in 2002. The business news remained rather gloomy. The trauma of the 9/11 World Trade Center attack and its aftermaths lingered. The "dot.com bubble" had burst with financial repercussions around the world. Business closures and bankruptcies were reported, often overshadowed by the financial scandals of Enron, WorldCom, Adelphia Communications and Arthur Andersen.

Business and investor confidence had eroded. Many companies and their executives were accused of fraud for manipulating investors, and misusing shareholders' money. The Securities and Exchange Commission had levied large fines on several banks and investment firms for misleading investors. Soon new regulations were issued enforcing investor protections. The business atmosphere was reminiscent of the earlier Savings and Loan crisis, but with an emphasis on "Irrational Exuberance" as expressed by Economics Professor Robert J. Shiller in 2000. Could this down moment offer new investment opportunities?

I had recently concluded my representation of IBUS Investment Group, a private real estate investor from Holland. We had opportunistically acquired more than a dozen distressed commercial property investments in the post-recession 1990s. Over the 1999 to 2002 period, the properties were sold to domestic investors as markets had strengthened. The sale of the Washington, DC properties in early 2002 led to a closing dinner toasting a rewarding 10-year relationship.

In this post-bubble period, executive office suites and similar shorter term office rental programs were overwhelmed by the sudden disappearance of their dot.com renters. U.S. units of Regus and HQ Workspaces had filed for bankruptcy. I thought, "Is it the time for a new venture in office space?" I reached out to friends and broker contacts. I visited similar nearby operations.

In early January 2003, a local friend approached me at a Rotary Club luncheon. "Frank, confidentially, I know of a business you might want to inquire about. A friend of mine owns Corporate Executive Offices, an 'executive office suite' at Two Sound View Drive, in downtown Greenwich. He has had a heart attack and needs to retire. He wishes to discreetly sell the business to a qualified operator without any publicity or future obligations."

"Tell me more." I spoke. "Are there any problems? Regus and HQ just went bust."

"No, none. He has been privately networking with some wealthy friends at the Belle Haven Country Club. A few expressed interest and a couple of offers surfaced. Both proposals were presented by a father as an investment venture for a young son with limited business experience, none in real estate."

He added, "The landlord rejected the proposals as they failed to satisfy the threshold business experience requirements to allow for a transfer of the lease obligation to either prospect as the business owner and tenant in the building."

After a brief thought I said, "Sounds interesting. I can certainly demonstrate the business experience. I just concluded a successful ten-year, commercial property investment program with a Dutch group. We just closed the last sale. But I'll need a qualified intermediary."

New Business Venture - Serviced Executive Office Suites

The business involved this relatively new concept in office services as a major tenant in a prominent Greenwich building, once owned by a former client in my earlier career. I was introduced to a prominent commercial broker, who arranged a meeting with the owner.

This early, private discussion led to mutual expressions of interest. The owner furnished a strict Non-Disclosure Agreement (NDA) for review prior to any further exchange of information. I responded that, upon review, I would be signing for my business, McBrearity & Co., Inc., which was started in 1991.

The target was an established business with a 15-year history and a well-known, stable roster of rental clients. My real estate experience and prior relationships with the landlord, and a prior landlord, would ease critical concerns and satisfy the landlord's business experience requirements for a transfer of the lease. The transaction could possibly be completed quickly and quietly, as desired by all.

I was jogging through Waveny Park in New Canaan a few days later when a good friend caught my attention near the soccer fields. He soon asked, "What are you planning to do now that you've closed out business with the Dutch client?"

"Well, I'm not planning to retire yet. I've been alerted to a business situation in Downtown Greenwich that could be interesting and might appeal to my son if he wants to do something new after volunteering in Africa," I replied.

"Is it a big money deal, or a small business?" He asked.

"I would say it's in the small business realm, local, services, not 24/7."

The word got around very quickly. Unexpected phone calls came in from numerous long-term friends in our New Canaan community. Some expressed quite serious interest. The Waveny friend soon wanted a "major" interest, a surprising request at such an early stage. I had not even identified the business.

Another good friend called as the word was circulating. He

sought to diversify family investments with some local business interests. He and his wife were loyal friends and frequent dinner guests over 15 years. Finally, another friend pressed hard to participate. He was also a long-term friend with many shared interests and relationships. It was not clear how he learned of any earlier conversations.

At this point, I had to sign the Non-Disclosure Agreement (NDA), as President of McBrearity & Co., and have my broker deliver it back to the owner before any new conversations occurred. I would provide copies of the signed NDA to all serious contacts before any specifics were revealed. The owner had stressed he did not want anyone to know the business was for sale.

I was taken aback by this unusual display of interest by my New Canaan friends. Several others seemed to be lingering around, asking questions. I had never reached out to these friends on personal business topics. Our collective focus was families, children, school, and community support endeavors, not investment deals together. My investment experiences involved advising U.S. pension funds and some international entities on large commercial investments, not local deals.

While I was flattered by their curiosity, I had not contemplated partners or "outside" investors. I was not sure it was needed. I had no detailed information to review or evaluate yet. I did not even have the basics of a deal. What was going on with my friends? I did not quite understand.

Friendships. I had been a member of the Rotary Club, and Board Member of the New Canaan United Way for several years. Yet, the enduring friendships in New Canaan developed from participation in the family interactions in our Catholic Church community, and the shared involvement with the programs of the local schools and town organizations over almost 20 years.

The families enjoyed many annual festivities. While all four of us were in our 60's, and in some form of "retirement", we were basically town friends. None of the eager-three had any experience in commercial real estate. One had a career in construction. Another had been a corporate lawyer with a conglomerate. The third had a career in marketing and was an avid golfer at a prominent local club.

After a brief review of early, public information in February, the three agreed they had some preliminary interest in this investment idea, subject to further review of operational information, financial statements, the landlord's lease, and other such due diligence items. Two of us had experience with First County Bank, which seemed to be a logical choice for any bank financing, if needed.

The actual owner of the business in early 2003 was Pyramid Executive Offices & Services, Inc. (with the selling individual as sole shareholder). By the end of February, in response to the signed NDA, the owner had provided a comprehensive history of Pyramid's operations, the lease, rental clients, employees, contracts, vendors, financials and his own assessment of business value. All the data and information were shared with the prospective partners, under the confidentiality restrictions of the NDA.

The Business. Conceived in the mid-1980's by a Greenwich real estate investor, the business Corporate Executive Offices, or CEO, offered a local version of the Regus and HQ Workspaces format of the period. No such high-quality, privately managed flexible office space options were available in Greenwich to respond to the specialized needs of its affluent corporate, financial, and entrepreneurial executives. The Regus and HQ formats set an early model for furnished, executive-style office suites with a "corporate" atmosphere offered under somewhat flexible and customized occupancy, or license, agreements.

It was opened in 1988 as a tenant in Two Greenwich Plaza at the Metro North Station. The business was sold in 1991. The second owner, Pyramid, relocated the business in 1999 to Two Sound View Drive, across from the station, under a long-term sublease from Citibank through 2009, with a five-year renewal option. Citibank had recently consolidated local activities and relocated operations to a nearby building.

The leased space totaled 16,100 sq. ft., including the whole first floor at the lobby, and part of the third, representing 54 offices of varying sizes along a generous window line on both floors. The business offered furnished offices, conference rooms, staffed reception area, and related amenities in a well-equipped format, enhanced by professional services and administrative support.

For a monthly fee, clients (licensees) rented the private office or offices, typically under a one-year license agreement, known as a Services Agreement. The total monthly rate included charges for the office(s), telephone(s) and assigned local phone number(s), fax modem line, television and internet connection(s), and four hours of meeting room time. The monthly fee covered support services such as call answering, mail handling and distribution, coffee, and access to cafe areas.

Other ala-cart services were provided for additional charges as detailed in the Services Agreement. In addition, the business supported a large "virtual" clientele (Identity Clients) seeking, for a monthly fee, a genuine Greenwich business address and phone number plus call-answering, mail services and conference room access, without the need for a full-time office.

The business was a very profitable and admired enterprise that served two market segments: 1)"baby boomers" and 2) major corporations. Baby Boomers were male and female professionals, born after WW II, with established careers in financial services, publishing, marketing, consulting, insurance, and other sectors, who had made a life-style decision to conduct their books-of-business closer to home. Many clients were "emeritus" executives with their firms.

They chose CEO (and Greenwich) because it provided all the services and professional environment of their prior location (typically NYC) without the necessity of a big lease commitment, furniture purchases, technology anxieties, and other related costs. In the early 2000's period, Baby Boomers were a very prominent and growing force in the Greenwich economy, and surrounding areas.

In the immediate "Post 9/11" period, many Manhattan-based organizations sought "emergency" office arrangements for their senior executives in the event of another terrorist attack or a similar catastrophic disruption. Several offices were licensed to New York companies for this reason.

In addition, certain types of businesses were required by Connecticut law to have a legitimate physical business address in Connecticut in order to legally conduct any business in the state. A growing number of firms set up fully equipped, but rarely used, offices at CEO to comply with this Connecticut requirement.

I did my own analysis of the business and made my assessment of a fair purchase price for a well-established service business, including input from accountants as to market ratios and guidelines. A purchase price of $1.5 million was set based on the 2003 revenue level and future growth potentials. The business' client roster had numerous recognizable companies, and notable business professionals. Many had a long association with the business.

The seller and its counsel were submitting my background and the prospective Limited Liability Company (LLC) format, with four possible partners (to be identified as "Members"), to the Two Sound View landlord for preliminary approval. Everything was reviewed frequently, and confidentially, with the three friends during this pre-acquisition phase.

Members. During this period, we had regular meetings in a kitchen or family room where we reviewed the offering, due diligence materials, the lease, and projections all under the confidentiality requirements of the NDA. The issue of financing from First County and a loan guarantee surfaced. The prospective Members declined to participate in any such guarantee. That would fall to me, the "Managing Member."

In early April 2003, I signed a Letter of Intent (LOI), on behalf of a yet unfunded entity, with Pyramid Executive Offices & Services, Inc. to purchase the business for $1.5 million, subject to another 30 to 60 days of onsite due diligence to confirm all the numbers and information provided under the confidentiality agreement. A closing was tentatively scheduled for late May or early June.

Within a few days of signing the LOI, information about the pending transaction was all over the Greenwich real estate community. The seller, seller's counsel and our lawyer were enraged at the widespread disclosures and the unmistakable violation of the strict NDA by someone.

The owner reported through counsel that at one point he had as many as ten brokers congregated in the reception area wanting to know what was going on. I was repeatedly asked by the lawyers: "Who are these broker guys? How do they know so much?" One added, "Find them and shut them up. They are killing your deal." Then he added, "Pyramid is preparing to sue you."

"I don't know who they are," I replied repeatedly. "I don't know them or how anyone would have any information. Does the owner know them? What about his friends, or previous contacts? Have they played any role?" I got no reply.

When it was determined that the two shell entities that signed the early documents had no money, and the prospective ownership entity was not fully formed, potential legal actions ended. Pyramid then initiated a deliberate due diligence stall, slowly responding to data requests, and delaying access to onsite information and meetings with staff, licensees, vendors, and others.

The late May closing did not occur until late October 2003. In the interim, the owner collected his salary and benefits plus the cash flow and tax benefits for that period. The eventual CEO of

Greenwich, LLC had legal fees greater than anything budgeted. The aggregate costs exceeded $200,000, resulting in an effective purchase price more than 15% higher than planned.

The three Members claimed no real estate contacts in Greenwich and had no explanation for the disclosures. We did not know who these brokers were, or from whom they got such sensitive information.

The Members had little, if any, experience with a venture of this type. The new ownership entity was in the form of a Limited Liability Company. A Limited Liability Company (LLC) is a corporate structure permitted under state statutes, whereby the owners are not personally liable for the company's debts or liabilities. The owners (partners) are called Members.

LLCs are hybrid entities that combine the characteristics of a corporation with those of a partnership but require articles of organization to be filed with the state. The format offers the availability of flow-through taxation to the members, as in a partnership. An LLC is much easier to set up than a corporation and provides more flexibility.

The LLC Operating Agreement, earlier reviewed and signed by each Member, detailed the legal, management, and decision processes and obligations of the Members and Managing Member in accordance with Connecticut statutes.

Other technical and administrative factors were reviewed and discussed in acquisition meetings. The CEO clients' license agreements, which conferred occupancy and service commitments subject to fees and related provisions, legally established the clients as licensees, not rental tenants under a lease, with only those specific rights detailed in the respective Services Agreements.

Finally, the salary and benefits earned by the owner, as the chief executive of Pyramid (the business), were reviewed by a small business compensation consultant. The consultant confirmed that the compensation package was consistent with the industry's business standards. These executive compensation elements would continue for the Managing Member in the new LLC format.

Many concerns discussed in the pre-acquisition meetings with legal and accounting advisors periodically re-emerged. Pyramid was a corporate entity with a corporate accounting format. The CEO entity was an LLC with special accounting classifications for certain items, particularly the compensation and expenses of the Managing Member, who was technically not an employee.

As a result, the amounts in the CEO financial reports would be consistent with the projections derived from the Pyramid data, but certain items would be classified differently in the LLC's financials as reviewed and approved by the CPA. Other operational questions arose in meetings after the closing: insurance, bank relations, QuickBooks reports, and other matters under the control of the Managing Member. At times, they were referred to the experts: Neil Berkow and Chris Eck, CPAs with Berkow, Schechter & Co; Tom McKiernan at Abercrombie, Burns and McKiernan, insurance agents; and Jim Gareau at First County Bank.

Meetings. The LLC had quarterly Members' meetings beginning in early 2004. The Managing Member wanted to have all such meetings at Two Sound View, with easy access to any supplemental information. The other Members soon rejected that preference, favoring more convenient evening meetings near homes in New Canaan. These more informal meetings covered rental revenues, occupancy levels, financials, and other quick updates.

At the first Members' meeting in 2004, the Managing Member presented the QuickBooks report showing the results since the October closing. The numbers were strong, and cash flow was consistent with projections. Everyone was pleased.

A Member asked, "When can we start getting distributions? Results are good."

Another added, "No reason to wait on this!"

After a pause, I responded, "Wait a minute here. We closed four and a half months later than planned. We had unexpected legal fees. I do not know how that happened. How did such confidential information get out? Can anyone tell me? We lost four months of revenue. My priority now is to try to pay down the loan I have guaranteed. There is some modest amortization in the monthly payments, but still a big personal liability."

The Members replied, "Business is good. Let us get some early returns on our investment. We can deal with First County later."

I reluctantly deferred to the three Members on this decision with the reminder, "I am personally on the line here, this subject will not go away." After some procrastination, we issued the first CEO distribution in late June 2004. It totaled $35,000, after adjustments for contingencies.

Friends with Benefits.   At the same time, the three months of 2003 financial data for CEO of Greenwich, LLC were submitted to Berkow, Schechter & Co. for the preparation of the 2003 state and federal income tax returns. A component of the data was the balance sheet statement of the assets acquired from Pyramid Executive Offices & Services, Inc., specifically the fixed assets.

Chris Eck called to provide an update. "Frank, the seller had some surprising asset valuations on this Pyramid balance sheet. Was this ever discussed?"

"No, I got no response to questions about the financial statements. Little was shared on this subject," I replied. "But I do know he was an accountant and had been a corporate controller in his career before Pyramid. Is something wrong?"

"Well, I'm not sure. The Pyramid financials show large leasehold assets and leasehold improvements, in addition to furniture, equipment, and other standard property items. It's the leasehold asset valuations that seem unusually large."

"The Pyramid business had taken over a Citibank lease in the late 1990s as Citi was moving to another building. As a subtenant the rent goes to Citibank. I suspect Citi had negotiated a favorable lease deal with the then landlord. By the time the Pyramid subtenant stepped in the rent obligation was well below the market. The accountant/owner probably calculated this difference as an asset valuation to inflate balance sheet assets. I'm not sure, but what's the concern?"

"These assets are subject to depreciation over the lease term. These deductions on the tax returns will be relatively large, creating lower income, or a loss, for tax purposes even though the pre-tax income and cash flow are strong. It suggests to me that the ownership may have created something of a 'tax shelter' for his benefit. In the LLC format, it will now flow directly to the members."

"Let's keep this to ourselves," I replied. "We'll soon see how things play out when we have the tax returns reviewed and filed. But thanks for the heads up."

The favorable performance of the business, early distributions, and high occupancy began to circulate through the Greenwich brokerage community in late 2004 and into 2005. I became alarmed and angry once again. Some clients learned of the commentary and resisted rent increases, or simply refused.

As I inquired, it was apparent that someone was providing regular updates on CEO which became material for broker gossip. What was going on? I had to find out. I called my broker. "Did you ever determine who this broker group was and how they knew so much? It's starting to happen all over again."

"Well, these brokers network everywhere from business seminars to private clubs," he replied. "But I don't know how anyone would have such information on CEO's operations."

"Stay on the alert. This problem is resurfacing. Thanks for the help."

As events progressed, I had recurring brief discussions with two of the Members at random neighborhood activities in New Canaan. They would spot me as I was browsing the farmers' market or leaving St. Aloysius Church on Sunday morning.

"Frank, what's new at CEO?" They would ask.

"Not much since we last talked. Some landlords are inquiring about our expansion interests, and I have had some brief investor inquiries and discussions. Otherwise, nothing new. The building is the same. Business is strong."

One responded. "Well, we heard some brief concerns about the Sound View building from clients at the recent open-house: leaks, elevator problems, needed updates. Walking around we saw no evidence of any work at all. So, please keep us posted on things. We want to be part of the process. Okay?"

These random inquiries also occurred at evening events or neighborhood parties as a Member would pull me aside for an update. Questions often implied I was not keeping the Members fully informed, and he was charged with probing further.

I tried to preempt this variety of behind-the-scenes questions, comments and assertions with the regular quarterly meetings, financial reports, client status lists, backup documentation, and distributions benefiting from the special tax deductions acquired from Pyramid's balance sheet. It was full disclosure.

In these meetings I often added: "You guys are welcome to come down to Greenwich any time if anybody has particular concerns or questions. You all have all the reports and tax returns. I am in the office every day. It's full disclosure." No Member had ever dropped in for a visit after late 2003.

It soon became clear that the Members regarded CEO as a simple, relatively passive business that could be easily managed. They often asked, "Why do you go to Greenwich every day?" I emphasized, "This is not a real estate investment. It is a day-to-day, quasi-retail, office services business, with high-end clientele. It needs ownership's management presence on site."

In the ensuing months, the CEO business remained a quiet topic of interest among brokers and others in the Greenwich community. With the troublesome memories of 2003-04 revived, it was time to have a long-deferred meeting of the Members on serious LLC issues: confidentiality, the role of the Managing Member and procedures for major decisions.

While these key provisions in the LLC's formal Operating Agreement had been reviewed earlier, I arranged for an independent legal advisor to re-explain these provisions carefully and authoritatively to the Members in early 2006.

In response, a senior partner with Whitman, Breed, Abbott & Morgan hosted the Members in his firm's conference room in Greenwich, and began a very straightforward presentation, highlighted by the following:

- The Limited Liability Company (LLC) is a private business formed by and for the benefit of the Members. Members have a fiduciary responsibility for sensitive information, decisions, and actions. The LLC is a private enterprise.
- The Managing Member is responsible for the day-to-day decisions of the business and all operational and administrative functions, including meetings and financial reports.
- Major Decisions requiring the participation of all the Members are the following: investment capital, recapitalization, Member departures, new Member introductions, and capital call responses. He reminded everyone that the Managing Member is the personal guarantor of the LLC's financing, at Members' insistence. The Members must keep this in mind.

The Members acknowledged all the comments without any

questions. Efforts to engage the Members on confidentiality and the brokers' awareness of CEO got no response or discussion. The meeting ended quietly as the Members departed.

Demand Grows - Serviced Office Suites and Booming Boomers.

Greenwich was a fast-growing base of successful financial firms, particularly in the hedge fund and private equity sector. As a result, companies in investment, and boutique entrepreneurial sectors sought an outpost with proximity to these expanding firms, without a major lease obligation.

Many such organizations licensed offices at CEO in this period including Ann Taylor, Charles Schwab, Harrow Sports, Hearst Publishing, Merrill Lynch and Wells Fargo, among others. In addition, semi-retired baby-boomers, emeritus executives, and financial organizations continued seeking cost-effective, flexible, and well-staffed office arrangements.

The business grew significantly through 2006, with revenues up by more than 30% since late 2003. Vacancies declined, and office choices for inquiring prospects became more limited. As discrete broker inquiries continued through 2006, the thought of an expansion became more relevant, particularly with the early, unexpected, expression of interest by the Greenwich Office Park management team.

The convergence of these growth factors prompted the initiation of discussions with the LLC Members to explore expansion options, such as Greenwich Office Park, and recapitalization potentials to enable a response to this increased level of demand from a more secure financial base.

The LLC's real estate broker was asked to quietly respond to the earlier invitation from Greenwich Office Park to become a tenant. The Park's ownership had expressed a desire to have a new, high quality, complementary office service in the Park. Also, selected bankers were contacted for leads to local investors with possible investment interests. Discussions soon advanced on both initiatives.

Member distributions continued, increasing slightly in 2006. The inflated asset base from the Pyramid balance sheet elevated the LLC's income tax deductions, which resulted in tax losses, rendering the Member distributions largely tax-free with some losses applicable to other passive income.

At the Beginning -Two Sound View Drive

The 38,000 sq. ft. office building occupied a prominent downtown site with easy access to Greenwich Avenue shopping and restaurants, the Metro North train station, and major highways. Built in the late 1970's, it had a long history of corporate tenancy and experienced institutional ownership. The Hines Interests of New York and Houston owned and managed the property through the 1990's. The building was now owned by a local investment group.

Aside from Corporate Executive Offices, the other large tenant in Two Sound View was the Fairfield Greenwich Group, a financial firm founded in 1983 by Walter Noel, Jr. a prominent Greenwich resident. Fairfield Greenwich had merged with a local brokerage firm and began offering clients access to feeder funds of single-strategy trading managers, and hedge funds. The firm moved its headquarters to New York City in the 1990s, but retained its third-floor office of 10,000 sq. ft.

Now some 30 years old, few mechanical system upgrades, or capital reinvestment projects had been undertaken since the Hines ownership. Two Sound View was still a desired location, but somewhat known for air conditioning interruptions, leakages, and other bothersome malfunctions. The private, subterranean parking area had occasional flood episodes, chemical leaks from ceiling pipes, and garage doors that closed unexpectedly on an automobile.

The ownership and its building engineers were carefully controlling and managing these age-related deficiencies. We were aware of the frequent appearance of electrical, HVAC, roofing, and elevator contractors, but no notable projects were ever initiated. My staff and I were regularly responding to worrisome complaints and criticisms from clients without any Landlord participation.

To a large extent, CEO's financial performance was in response to a strong local and national economy which was also driving up real estate values, rent levels and related occupancy costs. It was a demanding time, knowing that Two Sound View's maintenance deficiencies could have a serious impact going forward.

Contingency Plan. I reached out to our broker again. "Business is good but I am concerned about the physical and atmospheric compatibility of the building going forward. The building has issues. Little has been done in several years. I do not want these deficiencies to hamper business. Could you quietly revisit the Greenwich Office Park invitation without it getting back to the Landlord?"

"No problem, Frank, I'll get right on it. Very confidential. Got it."

We had regular quarterly meetings, but I called two Members' meetings at Two Sound View in the summer and fall of 2006 to discuss these concerns about the building and the Landlord. We had had few meetings at the building. So, I walked the Members around at both meetings. I needed to make them aware of the building's condition and the potential impacts on clients.

"Guys, we have our annual CEO Xmas Luncheon in early December. I want you to casually network with clients and staff about everything: business, the building, clients, whatever. Get their views on the situation here at Two Sound View. OK?"

"We welcome the occasion," was the collective reply.

"Also, I have authorized our broker to discreetly survey the Greenwich office market for any opportunities for attractive rent deals in the 15,000 sq. ft. area. We want to get informed, without any exposure. I don't want to unnerve the Two Sound View Landlord in advance of renewal discussions."

I soon added, "This is all very confidential. I have also discussed these matters with First County Bank officials to keep them fully informed. The First County team clearly understood the situation, but also expressed their concern about CEO's capitalization, financial resources, and reserves. One actually looked at me and said, 'You've been making regular distributions from the beginning. What does the LLC have in reserve? You are the guarantor!' This is his big concern."

In fact, they had recommended contacting a long-term banking client who had expressed an interest in developing an executive office suite and service business in his office complex in Stamford. The Bank's client owned a nearby Corporate Park with 13 buildings and more than 600,000 sq. ft. of office space.

"One last thing," I said. "I will be reaching out to other financial sources for options to ease the financial demands of expanding and growing the business. I know of possible investors and other office suite operators who might be responsive to an investment opportunity and/or a joint venture in this growing business sector. Any thoughts on this?"

The three nodded, but nothing was said. So ended our early October 2006 meeting on this quiet moment.

I promptly contacted the recommended party. The bankers had advised that he had expressed an interest in this business format to add a new element to his office park. We met first at his office where we exchanged information and he brought attention to the varied space options in his Corporate Park. We met later at Two Sound View so he could see the space, atmosphere, and client roster in person.

A couple weeks later our broker called. "I think I have a good fit for CEO in Greenwich Office Park. It is a suite at the top of Building 2 overlooking the Park. It has a generous window-line, and direct elevator access at the 3rd floor lobby."

"Press on, business is good. The wait list is growing."

He soon called back. "I am working with the project manager on this Suite 300 deal. The rent will be competitive. They seem eager. Shall I schedule a visit?"

"Please do. I need to see the space. Thanks."

Expansion - Greenwich Office Park

I had visited the Office Park in the late 1980s at the beginning of my new career with Landauer Associates, as President of Landauer Advisors a real estate advisor to pension funds and institutional investors. The Park had been built starting in the early 1970s and became the world headquarters of the United Parcel Service in 1975. Continental Can, Phelps Dodge and Ericson were other prominent occupants in that period.

In 1986, I had sought the advice of Greenwich Associates, a financial consultant to pension funds, to help Landauer define strategies to address the US pension industry's growing interest in commercial real estate assets. Greenwich Associates was a major tenant in Building 8. It was the very first place I had visited in Greenwich, having just moved to nearby New Canaan after my promotion from the Florida office in 1985.

The office park had been acquired by an Oregon state pension fund in 1997 through a direct investment account managed by Jones, Lang, Wootton Realty Advisors. The ownership entity,

Property ConnecticutOBJLW One Corporation was an Oregon corporation with its local address at 2 Greenwich Office Park. By 2007, Jones, Lang, Wootton had merged with LaSalle Partners to become Jones, Lang, LaSalle Realty Advisors.

We soon met with the Jones, Lang, LaSalle on-site Project Manager, along with their leasing brokers for a tour of Suite 300 in Building 2. As expected, it presented well: efficient and inviting, with several convenient amenities, easy access, and abundant parking. After we left the tour I said, "Let us get moving on this. Get a proposal, lease draft and any other documents."

I was busy at the CEO office several days later, still awaiting documents from our broker outlining the possible terms of a lease deal for the 14,752 sq. ft. at Suite 300. I soon had a call waiting from Greenwich Office Park: "Hello, who is this?"

"Hi Frank, this is me at GOP. I have a question for you. Who is this new, second broker? What has he to do with your plans? We have been talking with your primary broker, whom we know from earlier prospects he represented. Why is this new guy asking questions of our brokers as if he is representing you?"

I was shocked. "Believe me, this guy has nothing to do with me or CEO. I do not know what else to say. I've never met him, don't know him, and have no idea."

"Frank, what I have learned over the past week or so is that your partners are known as the 'gossip guys' by our leasing team, and other local brokers. One or more of your partners seems to be in contact with this particular broker making these inquiries."

She then added, "Everyone thinks your partners don't treat CEO business decisions as private or confidential. A minimum level of professional respect and privacy is expected in these types of discussions. We do not have it here. Jones, Lang's corporate counsel in Chicago is annoyed by this. I expect a tough NDA will be submitted for your signature before anything else occurs. I will let you know."

"I am sorry. I have counseled the partners frequently about confidentiality, but no luck. I may need to stop having meetings; or hold meetings with no sensitive information. Send what you need to send. We need to get started."

"Okay, I'll be back with the NDA. We will go from there. Take care," she said as she hung up.

The deal at Greenwich Office Park was progressing at a deliberate pace with documents under review by Steven Steinmetz, a law partner with Ivey, Barnum & O'Mara. The Non-Disclosure Agreement was signed. A draft lease agreement soon arrived, highlighted by a specific paragraph emphasizing that the Managing Member, by name, was to be the Landlord's sole Tenant contact person, and the only source of Tenant communications.

Sarah Snow, an Architect with Granoff Associates, and a veteran of architectural plans at the Office Park, was retained to begin space layouts and drawings. Loft Construction, from Stamford, was chosen to construct the installation once plans were approved by Tenant and Landlord, project costs agreed, and permits issued.

First County's prospective investor and I had met frequently in late 2006. His interest in CEO increased with every visit. The revenue growth, expansion potentials, client roster and service quality all fit his desire to broaden his park's reach to a more diverse clientele seeking a more contemporary environment.

"Frank, I would like to buy the business or, at a minimum, become a major capital partner in this growing office space services business. I want to meet with all your partners and make my pitch. I am impressed with the business, the client history, and the inviting format. I believe it has strong growth potentials in the right hands. Get us a meeting with your partners to move this ahead."

The Members were summoned to another meeting to bring everyone current on the strong market, building conditions and the ownership at Two Sound View. Revenue growth was averaging more than 10 percent per year since our purchase. Many more prospects were waiting for office availabilities. Given the uncertain management focus of the Two Sound View Landlord, I stated it was clearly time to advance discussions of a new location and a new capital source for an expansion of the business.

Business conditions were reported regularly, so the growth rates were no surprise. Each had received $30,000 in distributions in 2006. The Members had visited Greenwich Office Park. The Suite 300 availability in Building 2 generated a favorable response. The question was how to proceed to the next step.

I wanted to introduce the prospective investor as a well-capitalized entrepreneur with deep experience in the local office market, and an expressed interest in the CEO business format. He was endorsed by First County Bank.

This Members Meeting was convened in CEO's small executive conference room on the third floor at Two Sound View in order to keep everything private, and out of sight. The GOP option got prompt acceptance by all: a complimentary addition, great amenities, and good location. The Members recognized the economic efficiencies of the two locations: few additional staff are needed, and many technical, administrative, and marketing costs would be spread over the two locations. The new operating entity would be CEO of Greenwich II, LLC.

The Suite 300 space in Building 2 was a go, subject to the final letter of intent, lease review, space plan, construction contract, and the formal registration of the LLC Operating Agreement with the State of Connecticut. Given CEO's economic performance to date, First County would be receptive. The Members quickly agreed to be responsive to the Bank's requirements regarding capital, and the anticipated $700,000 letter-of-credit obligation of the lease.

The final agenda item, the discussion of a new outside investor and an in-person meeting with the candidate, went nowhere.

The Members had no interest in and felt no need to introduce new, outside capital, regardless of the experience, relevance, or quality of the source. It was a no, with no questions and little discussion, in contrast to the earlier items on the meeting's agenda. After a brief pause, I invited further comments. But the meeting ended with, "keep us posted on the Greenwich Office Park deal."

As the three departed, I had to contain any contentious response about keeping them posted. "I've signed a very restrictive confidentiality and non-disclosure agreement," I thought to myself. "How can I keep the 'gossips guys' posted on these sensitive details?" It was time to stop sharing so much and move on.

The GOP lease for 14,752 sq. ft. in Building 2 came together rather quickly, leading to a signing by both parties in March 2007. The agreement provided a ten-year term beginning in December 2007, with a $50 per sq. ft. initial annual rental rate. The space would contain 44 individual offices of varying sizes, a reception area, one large conference room and two smaller meeting rooms. The suite would have direct elevator access, a kitchen area, private restrooms, and a secure, temperature-controlled technology room for internet, phone, and television services. Costs were covered by the installation budget in the lease.

Two Sound View. In this period, we learned that a new investment group had acquired Two Sound View Drive in early 2007. It was a private, unannounced transaction. According to most sources, the office building was not on the market, and brokers were surprised. The affiliated entities included multiple LLCs. According to sources, the organizations were diversifying their property portfolios, shifting away from a retail/shopping center focus.

While suspicions had surfaced much earlier, a rather brief Estoppels Certificate confirming the new ownership arrived in early May 2007, well after the fact. As the largest tenant in the building with a lease subject to renewal in late 2009, we were shocked at the apparent lack of Tenant inquiry or property investigation.

We saw no evidence of pre-acquisition due diligence: no physical inspections or engineering assessments, no lease reviews, and no tenant interviews. It was clear to many that Two Sound View was purchased in a fast-rising market with little real investment analysis.

The new Landlord's management team rushed to make a strong impression. New shrubbery and flowers were planted in the Spring to enliven the landscaping. The lobby decor was enhanced with marble floors, travel posters and new entry doors. Tenants were relieved at the new owner's attention in the early summer.

However, everything stopped once the posters were hung. The restrooms on all three floors remained dark, dirty, and often cold. Elevators lurched floor to floor. Tenants coming up from the garage with wet shoes, quickly slipped on the slick marble floors. Soon the elaborate flooring was covered with rubberized mats.

Mechanical disruptions became more frequent. Chemical leaks from air conditioning units and related piping damaged shoes, briefcases, and anything else on an office floor. The pipes in ceiling areas often leaked over weekends leaving corridors and offices damp by Monday morning. The garage doors created almost daily anxiety.

The prior ownership and its building engineers had carefully controlled and managed these age-related deficiencies. The new Landlord's management team was not aware of, or prepared for, the critical property management effort now required, and had little experience addressing the atmospheric needs of a high-end, multi-tenant office building. I soon lost patience and scheduled a visit to the ownership and management offices. The business was enduring unacceptable distractions, interruptions, and client stress.

I confronted the Landlord's team to get some answers. "Guys, thanks for your time here. As you know from previous messages, CEO and its clients have some concerns at Two Sound View regarding building systems, garage flooding, HVAC leaks and other building problems. What are you doing to address these issues? It is now getting quite urgent."

"Frank, good timing," was the reply. "We have been studying these concerns since we bought the building. These problems exist throughout the building, in the ceilings especially, from the garage to the third floor."

"Yes, I think we know the scope for sure."

"Yes, but the technical solutions are hard to implement efficiently in a fully occupied building. The level of difficulty necessitates access to these ceiling and HVAC zones for extended periods to repair, replace, and test plumbing, drainage, and HVAC units. As a result, major sections of the building will need to be vacated so our engineers and contractors have ready access to the ceilings and floors across the building to implement the plan and complete all installations and improvements in the most efficient manner."

"Well, are you suggesting we leave, relocate elsewhere?" I asked.

"No, our thought is that CEO could consolidate on one side of the floor while we work on the other. Then we reverse the process to work where you were. These steps would enable an efficient execution without necessitating your departure."

"The first problem I have is that CEO is fully occupied. We have no offices to handle such relocations. Plus, our office clients each have their own independent businesses. Such an unexpected disruption will cause many to leave, go home, or relocate elsewhere. The revenue loss would be significant, and hard to recover."

"Well, I see the problem," he replied. "We will need to review these circumstances with our team to see how we could do this in stages over a longer period. We don't have that answer right now."

"Well, we could actually be talking about the CEO lease renewal at this time, not deferred maintenance. The lease will come due late 2009. We need to bring both these discussions to the table as soon as possible."

The meeting ended on that note. As I drove back to Greenwich it became clear again that CEO had a serious problem as the major Tenant in a neglected building with a seemingly inexperienced office building owner. At that moment, the reality of an expansion to Greenwich Office Park seemed very fortuitous.

Greenwich Chamber and Broad Outreach. With the pending total of 98 offices and two locations, it was time to focus on endeavors to broaden the exposure of Corporate Executive Offices, expand community outreach, broaden demographic exposure, and incorporate the latest internet elements to streamline everything.

Large advertising posters were installed in rented display panels at the Metro North Stations in Fairfield County. The well-illustrated and detailed message was uniform: *We Can Make a Difference!* with flexible, state-of-the-art, fully staffed workspace solutions *Now in Two Locations*. The panels produced many direct inquiries. The rental contracts ran to year end.

Morstad Associates, our public relations team, also recommended that the business would benefit significantly if the Managing Member had a larger personal presence in the Greenwich business community. Since CEO was already a member of the Greenwich Chamber of Commerce, the Managing Member soon became a Member of its Board of Directors.

This new role provided full engagement with the Committees involved with Town affairs and the Town's business scene. In addition, the CEO venues would often host Executive Sessions, along with various Committee meetings, creating new connections and positive interactions with the diverse business community.

Everything was positive in the mid-2007 Greenwich office market. The strong economy and tenant growth were driving rents higher. Revenue at CEO was also strong, indicating another 10 percent annual increase, or more. With few window offices available, and several clients expected to expand, choices were limited until the suite at GOP opened in October. If business continued in the current pattern, with a second installation of 44 more offices next year, CEO could experience an especially strong increase in annual revenue for 2008.

The space plan was approved. The building permit was issued. The build-out contract was signed, and construction quickly commenced. Stamford Office Furniture would be furnishing the conference rooms and reception area, along with some perimeter offices.

Our tech consultant, Emerge Technologies, was upgrading and modifying the phone systems in the CEO technology rooms so that all incoming calls would be answered at either location. CEO would now have two sets of dedicated phone numbers, one for each location, to eliminate the possibility of any confusion as to where the call should be directed.

I was on the Board of Directors of the Greenwich Chamber of Commerce and volunteering to help grow the Chamber's membership through the Membership Committee's initiatives. Many CEO clients were not Chamber members, and likely prospects for my attention.

The Board included the executives of major local businesses such as Moffly Media, Patriot Bank, Greenwich Hospital, and the Hyatt Hotel, along with Realtors, accountants, attorneys, and executives of non-profits.

As we entered the fourth quarter of 2007, everything was moving in a strong, positive direction. The new construction was on schedule and slightly under budget. Technology elements were being upgraded and expanded for both suites. Marketing was refined and redirected to larger and broader audiences. The role on the Chamber Board added to the exposure and interaction of CEO with the Greenwich business community. The local economy appeared robust. Many new prospects were emerging. On the surface, the outlook was positive.

Dark Clouds. While the Greenwich business community planned to celebrate its growth and stability this holiday season, unexpected alarms started to break through the post labor-day news reports. The stock market and home sales peaked in October. Over this period, the Federal Reserve expressed concerns about liquidity and financial confidence. The subprime mortgage market was imploding with perhaps far-reaching consequences to the financial sector. The national economy was teetering on a recession in the "housing bubble" aftermath.

The CEO December holiday party at Two Sound View endeavored to highlight its business expansion as new brochures were circulated along with beer, wine, appetizers, and other home-made delicacies. The attendees, including clients, Chamber members, and guests welcomed the upbeat atmosphere from CEO. The LLC Members socialized with clients and browsed through the building to check maintenance issues and any evidence of capital improvements. Nothing had changed. Clients drifted back and forth to their offices to stay current on the latest from CNN or Bloomberg News, asking "What's next?"

5. LESSONS - THE GREAT RECESSION

2008-2009 Small Business Terror - Anxiety Reigns

With the addition of new clients to the GOP suite in the fourth quarter, revenue grew by another 10% in 2007, even with all the background distractions. Inquiries into the new year continued as Wall Street veterans lined up for the new offices at Greenwich Office Park. Executive departures from Salomon Brothers (now part of Citicorp), Bear Stearns and others arrived to reset their careers as independent traders or investment managers.

Negative economic news continued to reverberate as potential new clients visited CEO. The national housing market faltered as the "housing bubble" burst and the mortgage market was unwinding. JPMorgan Chase acquired Bear Stearns with Federal assistance.

Yet, CEO's business in early 2008 was robust as traders, analysts and their colleagues retreated to Greenwich. The widespread range of office inquiries soon indicated that many New York financial firms were downsizing, or possibly preparing to close.

Revive Two Sound View Discussions. I soon called our broker. "We can no longer wait to hear from the Sound View Landlord about the lease renewal. We cannot risk losing the Two Sound View space in 2009. We must initiate renewal discussions, regardless of ownership's reluctance to address maintenance and obsolescence issues. We have 98 offices, multiple busy conference rooms, upgraded tech and strong demand. It is not the time for us to downsize."

"Frank, I've been waiting for your call," he replied. "The lease specifies the five-year renewal negotiation to commence one year in advance of the lease expiration. You are right on it. I will call them today."

"We are confronting a peak office market period with high rental rates in prime office locations. Make sure the Landlord understands we need written commitments for maintenance upgrades and capital improvements. Okay?"

"Understood, thanks."

As I am processing these challenging matters in April, I received the Landlord's first invoice for common-area expenses associated with building operations in 2007. As I quickly reviewed the details, I am struck by the cost for snow removal at the building. The total, more than $20,000, was substantially more than any such common-area expense in invoices from the prior landlord. Also, tenant parking was in the subterranean garage. The open, surface lot was quite small.

I immediately called the Landlord's office in Fairfield to inquire about the charge. The call was forwarded to the bookkeeper. I introduced myself and said, "I am a tenant at Two Sound View trying to understand the common-area charges in your recent invoice. The snow removal charge is unusually high. We have little outdoor surface parking, it is tiny. Can you please explain?"

She replied: "Sure, thank you for calling. We have one contractor for snow removal for all our properties. I total all of their charges for the period and distribute them evenly to the properties in the portfolio."

"Are these just office buildings?"

"No, mostly shopping centers in various locations. We may have one small office building recently added. I'm not sure."

"We may be that office building," I relied. "Your shopping centers have large, open-area parking lots necessitating regular extensive snow removal. Our parking at Two Sound View is sheltered below ground, with about 20 spaces outside. The situation is completely different from your large shopping centers."

"Oh, I'm sorry. We just handled these property charges as we have done before. I will check with management and get this corrected."

"Please do," I said.

Meanwhile, economic news continued negative, and worry was growing everywhere. Clients were staring at their screens all day. The national housing market grew weaker. Bank failures and corporate bankruptcies were reported. Many varied explanations surfaced, but the collapse of Bear Stearns and its aftermath suggested a crisis was looming. Older clients were starting to panic.

At CEO, new inquiries were increasing, and the business could be an unexpected beneficiary of this economic uncertainty and turmoil. We offered furnished, fully serviced offices, professional support, meeting rooms, and flexible rental terms. The refashioned website and broader marketing exposure enhanced the reach to the regional economy and Wall Street.

I called our broker. "I just talked with the Landlord's bookkeeper. She had invoiced the building more than $20,000 for last season's snow removal at Two Sound View."

"What, what snow removal? Did it really snow that much?"

"She is reviewing. This is their one office building. Everything else is shopping centers with big parking areas. In the meantime, do not let this distract from renewal discussions. Inquiries are strong and growing. This could be a record year now with two locations and 98 offices. I don't want anything to get in the way of the renewal."

"Frank, be careful with these guys okay, they have a weak reputation. I do not think they have any office management experience. And keep in mind the late 2009 rent going into 2010 will be in the $65 to $70/sq. ft. area based on the 2008 market, up from the mid-$50s now."

"I know, that's a big jump. But what are the options? Attractive relocation choices are limited, and perhaps even more expensive with relocation costs and other factors. Should we wait, and be prepared to close Sound View next year? The business concept has a great future when I consider the technology changes, demographic shifts and other factors likely to surface in the near term."

"I agree Frank, it's a tough time for small businesses to be making these types of decisions. No question. I'll report back on the Landlord's response."

The worsening economic news persisted into the summer as the Federal government responded to the housing market crisis and mortgage loan defaults. The atmosphere of uncertainty and anxiety grew in the office. Talk of recession intensified. Some economists were leaning toward "very serious".

The broker called: "Frank, I believe we have agreement on rent for the five-year renewal. However, the Landlord believes that building operations, maintenance, atmospheric and safety standards are already covered in the existing lease agreement. They don't want to get into amending the contract unless CEO wants to negotiate a new ten-year lease deal."

"I'm having enough trouble with a five-year renewal as it is. The business atmosphere is very conflicted. We have an unusually high level of inquiry and visits, yet some old-timers are closing and retiring. Everyone is positive about CEO, but push for discounts, free rent periods, no extras for phone services, television connections, etc., and shorter initial terms. Many are weighing the real office format against the virtual office format. I can see high occupancy but weaker revenue growth in the near term."

"Frank, it's your call. I am not expecting any compensation from the Landlord, or you. I'd go with the accepted rent proposal, $68/sq. ft., and hope the building doesn't have any serious problems."

"Okay, get me the renewal agreement. Have Steve look at it. Subject to his comments, I will sign it promptly. We need to focus on marketing this one business now in two locations."

As we approached the fourth quarter of 2008, I intensified the focus on 2009 to reinforce continued growth into the new year. Morstad Associates arranged contacts with Hearst Communications, publishers of the Greenwich Time, Stamford Advocate, and other news publications in lower Connecticut.

I talked early with Peter Healy and his associates at Hearst to alert them to our planned twentieth anniversary celebration at CEO's early December Holiday Party. I also advised that we plan to have a brief cocktail party/open house for Greenwich Chamber members at CEO's new suite in Greenwich Office Park early next year.

Soon after the Labor Day weekend, families everywhere returned from vacation holidays refreshed and relaxed. In Greenwich, clients returned from Bermuda, Palm Beach, Nantucket, Martha's Vineyard, and the Hamptons to reconnect with businesses and colleagues. Children joined friends at the unique roster of public and private schools in Greenwich. The college crowd departed for the Ivy League and other top universities.

Crisis Emerges. Then, a series of unprecedented financial events brought business activity to a near halt, with a grim specter of looming economic upheaval. On September 15, 2008 Lehman Brothers went bankrupt after the Federal Reserve refused to guarantee loans. The stock market dropped. On September 16, the Federal Reserve took over American International Group. On September 21, Goldman Sachs and Morgan Stanley converted to bank holding companies to insure Federal Reserve protection. On September 26, Washington Mutual went bankrupt. On September 29, the House of Representatives initiated the $700 billion Troubled Asset Relief Program. Congress then passed the Emergency Economic Stabilization Act as markets fell further.

This barrage of shocking September news was daunting to everyone. "How did this happen? God, what's next?" Silence overtook the offices. Coffee consumption rose as clients stared out windows, and at their computer screens.

In response to this torrent of news, an emergency meeting was held at a Member's home in early October to discuss the pending financial crisis and its possible impact on the business of Corporate Executive Offices, now in two locations. All the Members were in attendance.

I emphasized the positive at the outset, "2008 will be a record year for the business, exceeding prior expectations. Everything is under control. We do have departures at Sound View, mostly the older regulars, but new clients and prospects are appearing almost daily. It is an unexpected rush. Look at our quarterly reports." Quarterly reports were handed out for review.

I added: "I have no insights as to the future economy, except that Greenwich is a center of financial businesses, financial services and executives in the financial sector. The impact on Greenwich and lower Fairfield County may be significant. However, with the client traffic exhibited in recent months, CEO could be a beneficiary of the turmoil and downsizing. But it's too early to tell."

Finally, "We plan to have a 20th year celebration at our annual Holiday Party, set for December 10. We will also celebrate Bill Day's 20th year with CEO. He is the client who was there at the beginning. Please come, it should be good."

A $50,000 capital call for CEO II was issued in November as a contingency for the transition to the new year. Two Members responded. One did not.

Back at the office the staff was talking. "What are we going to do?

People go back and forth to the kitchen in silence. Long-time clients have departed; gone home. Invoices are out. Mail is distributed. What's next?"

After some moments, I replied: "Ladies, we just need to sit tight for the time being. New clients are slowly moving in. Many proposals are awaiting responses. We can take this dull moment to plan for the holiday party in December, our 20th anniversary event. After two decades, we can get through this.

Anniversary and Holiday Party, 2008. With two months to plan and organize the December 10 event, the team delivered a timely and needed evening of hope and good cheer at Two Sound View. Clients from both locations, Chamber members, guests, vendors, and friends drifted in and out starting in late afternoon. A favored selection of beers and wines, an assortment of hors d'oeuvres, and tables of home-made desserts reinforced the festive atmosphere.

Staff writer Peter Healy, photographer Dru Nadler, and others from Hearst Communications arrived to gather insights on the venue, business model, its clients, and the latest local business mood. Bill Day's firm, the Day Group, received special attention as the client with the 20-year presence. Dru Nadler took photographs of the Holiday Party experiences.

As I watched the relaxed crowd mingle through the offices and the conference room cafes, a hand suddenly grabbed my shoulder. I turned. It was Pat. "How are you?" He asked. "Happy anniversary!"

"Pat, how are you, long time no see? Thanks for coming. Is everything okay?"

"It's been a rough year. My wife is seriously ill with MS. I had to close my advisory business. Everything has stopped. My brother and I are starting over."

"I'm so sorry. We have been wondering about you. Lots of voice-mail messages.

"We plan to get caught up on all that over the weekend. I'll have a full rent check to you on Monday."

He then added: "I also want to thank you for securing the office as you did. The office now contains almost all our valuable assets. We're quite grateful."

"No problem, Pat. We hope things get back on track very soon. Keep us posted."

Everyone wished Pat the best, and a Happy New Year.

Madoff Moments.   As CEO celebrated its 20th year, Andrew and Mark Madoff talked with Federal authorities about their father's massive 20-year Ponzi scheme.   Bernard Madoff, a well-known investor, and founder of Madoff Investment Securities controlled $65 billion on behalf of some 4,800 clients around the world. The whole enterprise was a "total lie" according to the sons. Bernard Madoff was arrested the following day.

The Madoff scandal was broadcast constantly, overshadowing other discouraging business and financial news of mid-December. Everyone was trying to understand the extent of these allegations. At the same time, clients and staff are awaiting Hearst's report on CEO and the anniversary event last week.

On Tuesday December 16, CEO dominated the first page of the business section of The Stamford Advocate with the message: "CEO benefits from financial turmoil", accented by a photograph of Bill Day in his office and the line "Variation on a Theme." The business, its history, clients, services, stability, recent expansion, and the variety of recent inquiries were all well described.

Unfortunately, Peter Healy's report was somewhat dwarfed by bigger, bolder headlines from Bloomberg News **"Fairfield Greenwich fund sent Madoff $7.3 billion"**, the Associated Press **"RBS reports link to Madoff fraud"** and other similar business news of that day. Similar versions of Peter Healy's coverage appeared in later editions of the New Canaan News and the Greenwich Time.

Our broker called from his Stamford office. "Hey, I saw the article in the Advocate, really good coverage for CEO. Except, it is surrounded by some bad stories of fraud and dishonesty in the investment world. How did you get placed in the middle of that stuff?"

"I don't know. These days it seems like any positive news is dragged down by some negative event. Maybe the Advocate wanted to reinforce 'Variation on a Theme'."

"Well, keep in mind that Fairfield Greenwich Group is a big tenant on the third floor at Two Sound View. That space may be coming on the market next year. No telling what the Landlord may do."

"Thanks, 25% of the building goes on the market. Just what we need."

A Members meeting was convened in mid-January to start the year. Financial reports are distributed documenting the strong revenue growth over the prior 12 months. Occupancy patterns and client lists were circulated, with my specific commentary: "These data reveal a much higher rate of turnover in the second half of 2008, and the rental rate discounts needed to secure timely replacements. We are now in a recession that is hurting businesses everywhere, and a revenue decline is likely in 2009, especially at CEO II in Greenwich Office Park. The recession's duration is very uncertain."

In response, capital calls were issued for both CEO entities: $40,000 for CEO, and $50,000 for CEO II. In addition, I advised "I will be approaching the two Landlords regarding 'rent relief' or lease restructurings. Office vacancies are mounting as the tenants close their businesses. The Landlords should be responsive. I will be making those calls shortly. You should be aware that new Non-Disclosure Agreements will be required, which will limit what details I can report."

All three Members rejected the funding request for CEO at Two

Sound View in its entirety. Two Members supported the CEO of Greenwich II request and funded $10,000 each. The third Member was dropping out completely. The Members' tone and reaction came as a surprise considering the record of distributions and huge tax deductions over the prior years.

I responded immediately. "Look guys, I am the guarantor here, as you demanded, and I must fund any shortfalls. You have had good distributions from the very beginning, and high tax deductions. My financial interest in the LLCs will grow as yours decline. You want to say goodbye? One Member is already gone. Is this how you wish to behave?"

After a pause, they responded: "We don't want to throw good money after bad."

I did not know how to react. "Ah, come to our cocktail party in late February for the Greenwich Chamber of Commerce. It will be a nice networking event, and you can see for yourselves the space and atmosphere and have a drink. We are arranging evening access to the suite through CBRE, and refreshments will be provided by the Park Cafe. It is for Chamber Members only, but you are invited. I'll get you cleared with CBRE."

While the Members did not attend, it was a lively Chamber crowd eager to visit, socialize and take in the space. As I wandered through the gathering, I spotted an uninvited stranger darting in-and-out of offices all around the suite. He was not socializing with anyone.

I caught up with him as he was signing his name to the roster before exiting. He turned to me, waved, and said, "nice build out" and left. The name on the roster was Adam Stark. He was not a Chamber Member, not invited, and not cleared to enter the building at these evening hours. Apparently, he snuck in and out.

Before long, the First County team called to get an update as the economic events unfolded. "Frank, how is everything? We are under some pressure to report on any business or lending issues. How are the CEOs doing?"

I repeated what I had been telling the Members. "Business is currently good but change and uncertainty are everywhere. Many new clients are signing up, but everyone now is on a budget. I will be talking with the landlords about this."

"How are your partners responding?" They asked.

"Not well," I replied. "The recent CEO Sound View capital call was rejected, and they forced a reduction of the recent CEO II funding call. One has dropped out. I am personally making up the deficiencies."

"Frank, this is ridiculous," they replied. "They've had good distributions and high tax deductions. They should be much more supportive. One dropped out immediately. This is a bit hard to take."

"I agree, but that's what happened. Business is good, but the overall economic scene has changed drastically, and everyone is terrified. I'm working hard to get through it."

"We know, Frank. We all must push through. Please keep us posted! Thanks." This tense reaction from First County, our lender, added to the anxiety and stress looming ahead.

I soon called our broker. "Hey, who is an Adam Stark? He came uninvited to our recent Greenwich Chamber cocktail hour at CEO, wandered all over the place, then left. Is he someone I should know about?"

"Frank, he's got an office suites business in White Plains, probably wanted to check out a competitor. He usually works through an agent in White Plains, a broker with CBRE."

"Thanks. A CBRE broker got him into the space after hours. He wasn't invited."

Meanwhile, an unprecedented roster of visits and inquiries from the financial sector kept everyone remarkably busy. At Two

Sound View, Aspect Capital, Greenwich Capital Management, Greer Anderson Family Advisors, Med Opportunity Partners and Raymond James Financial sought new offices. Greenwich Advisors arrived needing space for a team of seven.

At Greenwich Office Park, Highbridge Capital, Pennfield Capital, Freepoint Commodities and Reach Financial explored various office options as they assessed their needs. Tuck Bradford, formerly with Goldman Sachs, set up Mortgage Master, Inc. Bernard Jacobs Mellet Holdings, and Forstmann Little & Co. established Greenwich offices in the new CEO suite at the Office Park.

While the new clients arrived with partners or colleagues in tow, their business plans were not complete. Immediate budget considerations focused on rental rates, with the request to bundle all charges into one negotiated monthly rate.

These priorities directed them to the smaller less-expensive offices: some with two or three colleagues for a typical single-person office, or five or six colleagues for two adjoining single-person offices. The pace of change did not allow for a full reconfiguration of sections of the suite. However, new furniture and technology arrangements were installed to facilitate prompt occupancies.

Many of the new arrivals had established careers in investment banking and other varied financial organizations. Over the years, strong working relationships had developed with colleagues who had now relocated to the Midwest or West Coast to advance their careers with major regional players.

As a result, many new clients began networking by phone, e-mail, or video conferencing to revive these relationships and create an affiliation with a major regional firm. In return, the CEO client would provide the opportunity for the regional player to quickly establish a credible, secure new office in the east. This east-coast office would be headed by a known finance professional with existing Wall Street contacts and access to staff support, technology, and ample meeting spaces. The internet now connected everyone, everywhere, at any time.

In this flurry of new client inquiries and visits, mechanical disruptions continued to plague the Two Sound View building. Flooding from bursting ceiling pipes and chemical leaks from old air conditioning units were regular distractions. Staff arrived early on Mondays to inspect the premises for evidence of failures. The Landlord's maintenance crew often addressed these malfunctions over a weekend, without notice, leaving debris in rooms, and furniture often damaged. Despite prodding, nothing was ever fully resolved regarding Two Sound View's aged mechanical systems. The garage doors kept dropping unexpectedly, terrifying clients and damaging automobiles. The Landlord was largely unresponsive. The damage to one client's car is so extensive that a legal claim was quickly settled.

A ceiling leak in the garage deposited a day's worth of damaging chemicals on a Bentley owned by a long-time client. The chemicals caused shocking damage to the roof of the automobile, and other exterior surfaces. It was another legal claim quietly settled. The upgrade programs identified and discussed in 2007 were on hold or ignored.

Major national news crews descended on Two Sound View in the first weeks of April as detailed reports of the Madoff and Fairfield Greenwich Group relationship were made public and legal actions were initiated against Fairfield Greenwich. Some camera-ready team was on-site every day to catch a possible glimpse of the Noel family or its partners. First, it was CNBC with its emphasis on the financial scandal. CNN and NBC arrived intent on developing a broader perspective on the Noels and their clientele. The prominent Greenwich family had disappeared.

In the ensuing weeks, an atmosphere of gloom was pervasive. Downtown Greenwich was quiet. Fairfield Greenwich Group was out of business, and their 3rd floor offices, empty. Other tenants relocated elsewhere. The Landlord was soliciting CEO's larger clients for the 3rd floor suite at a below-market rent.

The recession reality was engulfing Greenwich and Fairfield County communities. It was an abrupt economic shock with unknown, longer-term repercussions. Management and staff reductions were reported at major corporate enterprises in the area. Retail business slowed precipitously, putting landlords and tenants at odds. New construction ceased.

For more than twenty years, Wall Street growth and banking expansions brought many new outposts to Greenwich and Fairfield County. Greenwich soon became a "hedge fund capital." Financial incentives from the State brought the Swiss bank UBS and Royal Bank of Scotland to new high-rise towers in Stamford. Uncertainty hovered over these financial businesses in the recession's aftermath. Some contraction had already occurred, a consequence of reductions in trading. Many Wall Street banking operations were scaling back to Manhattan because of more scrutiny, new regulations, technology innovations, and the changing economy. UBS and RBS in Stamford were particularly impacted by such forces, and their international implications.

Connecticut's tax revenue decline and the ensuing budget crisis was an immediate consequence of the recession. The State's budget dilemma placed unanticipated pressure on all aspects of government, especially the judicial system and the courts. Reports indicated that layoffs and retirements in the judicial branch, and the closing of courthouses to meet budget cuts, were having a negative impact on the quality of the State's judicial services. Anxiety was everywhere.

2009-2010 Resilience and Change

Many older, long-established clients at Sound View took briefcases, files, and fax machines home. Some shifted to "virtual client" status retaining phone numbers, voicemail, meeting space, and staff support. Several, such as Day Group, J.P. Logan & Co., and the Townsend Group, renewed. Younger, new clients, and visiting prospects, arrived with shoulder bags, cell-phones, CDs, and computers in hand to reignite careers in a new work-style format.

Demographic Changes. On October 24, 2005, the cover for Business Week magazine read: "Love Those Boomers! Their new attitudes and lifestyles are a marketers dream." This massive post-war generation that drove significant cultural and business trends for five decades continued to expand and refine how it wanted to live and work.

The "Baby Boomer" world totaled almost 80 million people, some 50 million households and an annual spending capacity of more than $2.0 trillion. By many measures, this generation was the most powerful consumer force in the economy and was likely to remain so for some time ahead.

The Boomers were an especially robust and engaging component of the Greenwich, CT economy. The demographic was redefining life after 50 years-of-age with second or third careers, rediscovering old skills and exploring new adventures. The Boomers were a major force of growth, driving up home prices in various locations, renting office space, and starting new boutique businesses.

The business of CEO flourished as this cohort expanded their businesses, investments, and philanthropic interests. The clientele was corporate, courteous, and circumspect. Individual private offices with corporate style desks, credenzas and file cabinets welcomed each such client who appreciated the familiar decor.

The male Boomer was clean shaven and typically attired in "Brooks Brothers' casual", an open collar shirt, a sweater or sports jacket. A tie in the office signaled a pending interview or client meeting. The female attire suggested Ann Taylor basics, perhaps with a touch of Ralph Lauren. The attire was routine "business casual" in the CEO Boomer world.

The clientele was dependent on CEO's facility and services: furniture, telephone answering and voicemail, fax machines, internet and tech support, mail delivery, conference rooms and free coffee. New clients routinely toured their spouses to show the office, services, and amenities. Rental costs were rarely an issue. The clients were very appreciative, with thoughtful gifts for staff at the annual party.

All this suddenly changed. On August 3, 2009, barely four years later, the Business Week headline read: "The Incredible Shrinking Boomer Economy." Companies across the country were scrambling to adjust as the free-spending generation that had powered the economy went on a budget. No one predicted or anticipated that an economic crisis would devastate and cripple a consumer base that had been a bulwark of the economy for most of five decades.

Few places in America felt the collapse more than Greenwich. Boomer consumption declined, investment activity ceased, and home values fell. Their business relationships frayed, and offices were abandoned. Business at CEO paused significantly as Boomers retrenched or departed. The quiet, sophisticated, and affluent roster of vital clients went ashen, despondent, and argumentative.

Concurrent with the shrinking Boomer spending capacity was the shrinkage of Wall Street powerhouses. Greenwich was inundated with former Wall Street traders, bankers, and investment advisors, unemployed and starting over. As a stream of soft-spoken Boomers exited CEO in an emotional but orderly manner, an assertive crowd of younger newcomers stumbled in looking for offices with the message "I've got to get out of the house!"

This Generation X clientele was vocal, boisterous, and presumptuous. Many claimed they do not need any help for anything. They already had everything. Sure, they needed furniture, but were prepared to bring in everything else. They do not get mail, it is e-mail. They answered their own phones. They brought a big, flat screen television into the offices to watch CNBC, 24/7.

When questioned, most acknowledged, "No business plan yet. I just need to get out of the house to focus and network." Agonizing meetings with Gen X prospects and their spouses often ended with, "Is this okay with you, Hon?"

Some factors required further acceptance by the CEO management team. The Gen X man had a multi-day growth of beard, and was typically attired in loose-fitting, well-worn jeans and a grey or black t-shirt. Most wore running shoes. On warm days, it was knee-length shorts and flip-flops.

The corresponding female attire suggested regular visits to J Brand, J Crew, DKNY or Lululemon. Dark, tight-fitting jeans or black leggings, and long loose-fitting grey sweaters or tunics described the female Gen X standard. Casual shoes with thick tall heels were suddenly an eye-catching sight in the office.

The Gen X crowd did not favor the traditional corporate office arrangements or decor and had no interest in single-person offices. Gen X preferred furniture, and equipment configurations, that provided a dual functionality: efficient, private tasking, along with easy collaboration with colleagues. In response, the CEO team converted a section of individual offices into larger "team" rooms for 6 to 12 people. Desks were reconfigured, or replaced, to accommodate the computers, internet, and television needs of the new clientele. The response was positive. Generation X was the new growth factor in the CEO business model.

Technology Advances. A commentator once wrote that when reviewing film footage of the 9/11 terrorist attack, he noted that the people of New York had no smart phones with which to personally record the horrifying events as they unfolded: "History may well look back on 9/11 as the world's last under-documented mega-event." And social-media communications were non-existent.

The population a decade later may resemble their earlier counterparts in many respects. However, when and where they communicate and relate to one another, and how and where they save their data, records and files has undergone a profound and permanent transformation.

This transformation had an equally fundamental impact on the business of CEO, its service format, and its base of clients. The typical client set-up in an office during the earlier 2000 period consisted of a digital handset phone, a single screen desktop computer (Dell or HP), a printer and a fax machine. The internet connection was CompuServe or AOL over the phone line.

The fax ran all the time. The desktop computer was for word processing, spreadsheet analyses and e-mail communications. Large reports, presentations and other such documents were delegated to CEO staff for more professional production. The client had a mobile phone, but it was rarely used in the office.

Veteran attorneys often sought the comfortable executive atmosphere with support staff and private meeting rooms. However, they discovered the added cost of a file room for confidential documents, case studies, court records and client correspondence would add significantly to the monthly cost of the desired office. Consequently, many sole practitioners became "virtual clients" with an address, mail service, and access to support staff and meeting rooms. But the work was done elsewhere.

By 2009, everything was changing for those up to the challenge. The fax machine was almost obsolete. The Xerox machine made copies and printed documents, and could now scan any document to a specific, private destination. The single screen on the earlier desktop was replaced by three screens for continuous multi-tasking. For many, a laptop added further continuity to a 24/7 world.

Everyone was addicted to cell phones with their convenience and inexpensive calling plans. The BlackBerry made an early entry into this zone, but the challenging keypad and unpredictable service drove many to other smart-phone choices. Dell and

HP products were replaced by Samsung, LG, and Toshiba. Apple devices began to appear everywhere.

At the same time, "the cloud" was becoming the reliable storage platform for public records, financial documents, court reports and case studies. Small legal practices now sought shared office arrangements with its convenience, support staff, advanced technology, and private conference rooms.

Traditional desks and file storage were little needed by the new technophiles. Everything had been scanned and dispatched to a hard drive or "the cloud." Sole practitioners with legal associates and their computers no longer needed large, secure file rooms for private records and document retention. A very welcome client group arrived in this time of change.

In this transition, CEO was a dual-office realm straddling the old and the new. While some older, long-term clients had upgraded to Windows 7, little else had changed. Some stayed with AOL well past its prime. Most persisted with the fax machine and the traditional phone handset for business communications.

The younger arrivals of 2009 brought a new perspective to the office atmosphere. The CEO handset phone was relegated to incoming calls answered by the office receptionist and directed to voicemail. Outgoing calls were made on the smart phones; one for business communications and selected responses to voicemail, and another for personal chats.

Public areas became a frenzy of activity, muffled talk and unexplained gestures as these clients walked the halls or lounged in meeting areas talking to business colleagues, family, or friends. The CEO suites were awash in screens and vivid colors as CNBC flashed across the walls and Bloomberg trading patterns undulated on the screens.

New client offices had at least three screens and a flat panel TV on all day. An expanded array of video conferencing formats added to a sense of instant connectivity. Responses to sudden news flashes were often quite vocal.

Much had been written about this technological revolution. At CEO, it all played out with rapid tech reinvestments and timely adjustments as Wall Street sank and the recession began. What had been a traditional, high-service environment for private, executive offices transformed to a high technology environment offering a mix of serviced offices, semi-private office clusters, flexible work zones, and co-working enclaves. And everyone was on a budget.

LESSON

The Sharing Economy

These multi-dimensional adjustments and modifications became the essence of a new economic model defined as peer-to-peer based activity providing or sharing access to services, information, and data. This evolving economic model is facilitated by internet platforms and business-to-business collaboration. Shared office spaces, and open co-working venues were an early factor in advancing the growing importance of the "Sharing Economy."

We read about "The Sharing Economy" as articles appeared in the New York Times, Wall Street Journal and even the Economist examining the various factors affecting this emergent economic force, its many elements and influences, and the need to remove obstacles to implementation and growth. We heard about Airbnb, SideCar, Lyft, and Uber, and the surprising responses from hotels, taxi, and limousine services. The commentary suggested a new phenomenon: "a great unforeseen benefit of the digital age", as stated in the Economist.

The business world should know that shared facilities, shared technology, and shared administrative support have been formidable elements of commercial office occupancy for many decades. The business center, the shared office suites and the co-working spaces were all early elements, now refined and enhanced by the internet and related technology.

In these thousands of establishments around the world, office space and supporting elements are shared. Conference rooms and video conferencing are shared amenities. Secure communication systems, internet services, collaboration rooms, and

HDTV access are all shared, not to overlook coffee and kitchen services all day long.

Clearly, the sharing economy has expanded well beyond office space needs. Demographic changes, lifestyle considerations, the digital world, and a "work anywhere anytime" culture have all converged to expand the measurable benefits of shared economic experiences, "a great unforeseen benefit of the digital age."

LESSON

The Transformation of Workspace

The convergence of demographics, the internet, technology, and necessary adjustments to the recession's impact, initiated a transformation of the workspace requirements for many. With social media, video-conferencing services, and the emergence of the sharing economy, workers, employed or unemployed, sought a wider array of workspace venues. Early explorers sought Starbucks, or local libraries. In time, worker needs, expectations and new disciplines prompted innovations leading to refined business centers, co-working suites, flex-space, collaboration zones and other formats in response to these new economic realities.

In the pre-recession period (2006-2009), researchers estimate that fewer than 100 co-working spaces existed in the United States. By the 2009-2010 period that total began growing exponentially. The recession, in many ways, was an abrupt, driving force. The commercial property market had weakened, and property owners found a new, unexpected source of tenancy.

Tenant/landlord deals were made as the co-working trend was accelerating across the country. As regional, national, and international trade organizations emerged, it was clear that serviced offices and co-working organizations would have a strong presence in the economy going forward.

Corporate Executive Offices had evolved significantly from its early introduction in 1988 as a full-service business center with very traditional executive office configurations, reinforced by the furniture, art, and decor of that corporate era.

Over time, the format responded to new customer requirements: larger offices for teams, more conference rooms and meeting spaces, more technology elements and services, and flex-space for virtual clients. Throughout this evolution, it retained a high quality, supportive atmosphere with careful attention to specific client needs, mail services, office administration, privacy, and security. It was a contemporary, professional business venue, never a social club.

2009-2010   Delay, Denial and Neglect

We learned in 2008 that ING Clarion had quietly replaced Jones, Lang, LaSalle as the Oregon pension fund's investment manager for Greenwich Office Park. Soon thereafter, it altered the GOP management and leasing structure. The prior manager had departed with little notice. The role was absorbed by CBRE, both for property management and leasing. A CBRE property management team was set up on site, and CBRE brokerage became the Park's exclusive leasing agent.

The new contact at Greenwich Office Park was a Lisa Andrews, the on-site manager reporting to a regional executive in ING Clarion's New York office. The new GOP management office remained on the first floor of Building 2, easy to reach from the CEO suite on the third floor.

Lease Restructurings. Overtures to revisit the lease and rent schedule began early in January with brief visits to her office. "Lisa, this recession has the potential to be very problematic, challenging for everyone. All the CEO clients seem to be starting over on a new, lower budget. Prospective client visits are frequent, occupancy is high, and the virtual roster is growing. On the surface it looks good. But no one will pay what we were getting in 2007 or early 2008. Long-term clients will not renew at the old rates. If this continues, both CEOs could be full and turning prospects away but not able to meet all operating expenses in the coming months, even after staff adjustments and other cuts. We may need some temporary accommodations to get through it."

"I understand, but we are not hearing this from others," she replied. "But I will talk to the New York office and get a meeting arranged as soon as possible."

"Thanks Lisa. All this is confidential. We signed a strict NDA in 2007."

The initial NDA was signed with Jones, Lang, LaSalle. Soon a new, quite specific Non-Disclosure Agreement was issued and executed by CEO of Greenwich II, LLC on February 17, and by the regional executive for ING Clarion Partners on February 18, 2009.

While brief chats occurred with Lisa to remind her of our January conversations, no response emerged. In March and April, CBRE brokers made unannounced visits to the third-floor suite to look around and get a sense of the space. The CEO staff asked, "Can we help. What are you looking for?"

"Oh, we have office prospects looking for temporary space and we want to check this out," was the ready reply.

After several such visits, I called her. "What is going on here, why these repeat visits by your brokers?"

"I'm so sorry, that should not be happening. I'll get it stopped."

We were told later that New York executives were angry over these unauthorized visits.

Serious discussions resumed in May with deliberations over a short-term remedy or a longer-term solution. The New York office was uncertain about what the ownership expects or how receptive the ownership might be to any modification. The comments suggested that the ownership believed the recession would be brief, with recovery soon. As a result, Clarion leaned toward a short-term modification.

Over the summer, CBRE brokers continued to visit at unexpected times, often after business hours. Clients working in the early evenings were caught unawares as a broker said hello, peered into their offices, or a conference room, often asking to see the secured tech room down the hall. On several occasions, the brokers were accompanied by unnamed visitors.

The following morning a client often asked, "What are these guys doing here at seven in the evening?" I could only reply, "I wish I knew."

In August, ING Clarion delivered the First Lease Amendment which offered a 44.4% reduction in monthly rent for a 14-month period beginning retroactively in March. However, Tenant would be obligated to repay all rent reduction amounts ("deferred rent"), plus interest, in a modified rent schedule for the remaining term.

The proposal was clearly a temporary remedy anticipating a prompt return to prior norms. It was not consistent with CEO's perspective, or that of others. The regional business world was experiencing dramatic changes driven by the stock market, home values, demographics, technology, and new life-style preferences.

Recent occurrences in the Office Park were examples. A London-based hedge fund leased a large second floor suite in Building 2, below CEO. The space was promptly reconfigured, equipped and finished for their arrival, which never happened. A large trading firm leased 20,000 sq. ft. in Building 5. It never took occupancy and located elsewhere. Similar occurrences were evident throughout Greenwich and in other nearby markets.

At that moment, CEO II had no practical options. The First Amendment was signed and approved in September. Payments were made accordingly. Quarterly financial reports were provided as required by the Amendment. The Letter of Credit remained unchanged.

Soon after Labor Day, it became clear that Greenwich was a vital haven of veteran traders and investment managers disengaged from lower Manhattan's financial core. Without any notoriety, Wall Street had begun reaching out to these alums to establish, and fund, satellite investment and trading entities, without adding to New York employment rolls or long-term lease obligations.

Suddenly, the CEOs became the base for American Global, Seaport Group, Odeon Capital, Jeffrey Matthews Financial, Venetus Partners, Sears Holding Management Co. (later, Seritage), Alicanto Capital and others. These firms followed in the earlier pattern set by Highbridge Capital, Mortgage Master and others, at both CEO and CEO II.

New prospects kept appearing, often without any notice. At Two Sound View one September afternoon, a group of three young men arrived in the reception area wishing to tour the CEO suite. They were seeking to relocate their business from suburban Westchester County to Greenwich for tax and business reasons.

A pair of offices at CEO Sound View would work, offering convenience and some tax relief. We provided a complete tour of both floors, available offices, parking, tech, and support staff. Brochures were provided with rental rates and terms for the offices of interest. They assured a prompt follow-up and proposal request.

After about ten days, we retrieved the business cards and called the office at 445 Hamilton Avenue in White Plains, NY, Suite 1102. A message was left on voicemail: "Please call back, we are awaiting your reply and office needs." After two additional messages, we moved on to other prospects.

As budget sensitive new clients sought the offices at Two Sound View, it became important to revisit the renewed lease and pre-recession rent obligations, as we had with Greenwich Office Park. The Landlord was receptive to a discussion, subject to a Confidentiality Agreement which was signed on November 1, 2009.

From CEO's perspective, the ensuing dialogue with the Landlord must also address maintenance and building upgrades as clients continued to complain about the upsetting Monday morning discoveries. Electrical interruptions were frequent, emanating from the neglected utility room deep in the garage below. Several clients were withholding rent as incentive to get maintenance changes instituted. Vacant space was now available in nearby buildings.

The Two Sound View Landlord had remained unresponsive to complaints. In response, Loft Construction, the contractor on the CEO II installation, volunteered to respond and correct the damaged ceiling panels, doors, flooring, and other repairs discovered after an episode, at no charge. Similarly, Emerge Technologies offered free tech assistance after electrical disturbances.

In the meantime, the Landlord submitted monthly invoices with unusually large increases for electricity usage and common-area expenses. After some investigation, it appeared the excess charges related to the vacant Fairfield Greenwich suite on the third floor. Some lights and all the HVAC units were on 24/7, and periodic housekeeping occurred for showings. For some reason, these expenses were allocated to the adjoining tenant, CEO.

History was repeating. I called the Landlord's bookkeeper. "Hi, it's me again calling from Two Sound View in Greenwich. I have a question about your recent common area charges to the CEO account."

"Yes, sure, how can I help?" She replied.

"Well, I've seen a large increase in electricity charges, HVAC expenses and cleaning costs. Everything has increased over the past few months. What's happened?"

"My records show you have increased your power usage and other activities on the third floor significantly. Is this not correct?" She responded.

"No, it is not. I think you are adding in charges that pertain to the now vacant Fairfield Greenwich suite. Can you check on this?"

"Well, we were told CEO was adding that suite to your business. Have you?"

"No, we have not. It is vacant, for lease. The ownership knows this. It's marketing it to my clients here. "

"Oh, then, I am misinformed here. Let me check, and get the invoice corrected. So sorry for the distraction." She replied.

"Thank you."

As 2009 ended, the frustrations intensified as both Landlords' perspectives were short term. The CEO business at Two Sound View was responding well to the economic challenges with revenue down by just 5%. Rent discounts, and some turnover impacted CEO II with revenue down by 25%, year to year. Overall, the business was down 12% from 2008.

The outlook for 2010 suggested a reversal of the two revenue growth patterns. CEO at Sound View would be down as new discounted rents kicked in across the entire client roster. Revenue at CEO II would climb sharply as free rent periods ended, discounts moderated, and a high occupancy prevailed. The projected year-to-year totals for the aggregate business could show little change.

Comprehensive big-picture Members Meetings were convened in September 2009 and January 2010 to inform all as to the issues and related challenges, to the extent permitted under the Non-Disclosure Agreements. The lease amendment proposal for CEO II was reviewed and discussed.

Economic implications and default risks were detailed. Client lists, quarterly reports, and annual financials for both CEOs were distributed. Data for the 2009 tax returns were detailed. At a certain point, the process was deemed "hopeless" by one Member. Another Member expressed repeated concern over "throwing good money after bad" in the weak economy.

Personal Financial Worries. As the anxiety of the exceedingly tense economic environment took hold, my wife and I worried that bankruptcy could be an issue. It was frequently cited in news and business reports. We sought to learn more details. We met with Attorney Steinmetz of Ivey, Barnum & O'Mara; and later with his colleagues who had specific exposure to the pros and cons.

The initial question was always, "Are you in default on any financial obligations?"

Our answer was, "No we're not. We just want to be fully informed. These are stressful economic times. I have a business confronting conflicting economic and cash flow factors, and a significant personal guarantee."

"How is the CEO business doing?" Was asked.

"The business, in terms of client activity and occupancy, is good, strong in fact. The problem is that everything has changed. Clients are all on new or revised budgets, forcing monthly rents down significantly from the 2008 levels."

"But your occupancy is good, what's the problem?"

"The problem is our Landlords are distracted or in denial. We are unable to get any meaningful response to our proposals for rent reductions and lease restructurings to deal with these new realities. The CEO LLCs' rent obligations have risen in accordance with the 2007 leases, while overall market rents have dropped, and office space vacancies have risen sharply everywhere. Our attorney and I are pressing hard with both Landlords, who seem to think CEO is in good shape. It's a big problem."

"I understand. Let me respond. Bankruptcy is usually a last resort option for most distressed financial situations. Moreover, serious negative consequences can overwhelm the apparent benefits. It can seriously damage your credit history. Such an event can appear on your public record, and negatively impact whatever else you might be doing, especially those negotiations with the Landlords."

"Then what do you suggest?" I asked.

"My thought is you should focus on the landlords, with rent adjustments and lease alterations, as you are doing, or possibly collaborative agreements that could benefit both parties as the economy recovers. A bankruptcy filing would likely end any such discussions."

"Thank you for your advice and observations. We will keep them in mind as we move ahead with the various negotiations."

2010 - 2011 Kicking Cans Down the Road

Few communications surfaced from the Two Sound View Landlord in early 2010. Tenant departures in their shopping centers and negative trends in the retail sector kept the Landlord distracted from Two Sound View concerns. Steve Steinmetz recommended Attorney David Rubin to advise on these potentially litigious situations. Attorney Rubin was soon provided documents related to both lease and rent negotiations, at Two Sound View and at Greenwich Office Park.

In addition, nothing was heard from the ING Clarion management team, except that the recession had little impact, "occupancy is high, rental rates are holding up, demand is good. No problems."

Other brokers, however, reported escalating vacancies as pre-recession tenants on 3 or 5-year leases were closing or moving elsewhere. Commercial brokerage commissions had all but vanished. The vacancy rate was approaching 25% or more. The small roster of new prospects sought smaller suites at much lower rents. CEO II might soon be the biggest active tenant in Greenwich Office Park.

In late March, a Yoav Cohen was in the Two Sound View reception area asking to meet me and visit the CEO office suite availabilities. He stated he was a financial consultant exploring temporary office space options for some Manhattan clients. Greenwich was a sought-after option with flexibility and convenience.

We initiated a comprehensive tour, during which he asked me directly, "Is this business for sale? Would you be interested?"

The completely unexpected question created a pause. "No, I'm not having those thoughts. My son, now working in Africa with the African Wildlife Foundation, may have a future interest. I don't know yet."

"Well, I may have clients with an interest. I'll let you know."

So ended the meeting. I retrieved his business card which showed he was with NYC Advisors, LLC with offices in midtown Manhattan, and White Plains at 445 Hamilton Avenue, Suite 1102. The latter address was familiar. "Who is this?"

After a few days, I could not contain the curiosity. I drove to White Plains to find out who occupied Suite 1102 at 445 Hamilton Avenue. To my surprise, it contained Adam Stark's office

FRANK B. MCBREARITY JR.

suite business, Stark Office Suites. "What is going on here? Are they interested in CEO as an acquisition? Just recently, John Robinson of American Global started getting mail from Stark. Why? This is bizarre, what do I do?", I thought to myself, as I drove back to Greenwich.

In April, the Members learned from me that ING Clarion was silent on a long-term lease restructuring after the execution of the First Lease Amendment. The Members conferred on a new proposal, and the necessary capital requirements in the short term.

In early June 2010, CEO of Greenwich II, LLC delivered a long-term proposal that addressed CEO's commitment to the lease, and the full recovery of any deferred rent over the remaining lease term. The proposed rent schedule started at $40 per sq. ft. As CEO was awaiting a response, transcripts of internal ING Clarion and CBRE communications and e-mails (later provided by Attorney Rubin) revealed the confusion, indecision, and procrastination in their deliberations:

January 20, 2009 - "Lisa communicates rent relief discussion start."

March 11, 2009 - "CBRE brokers got heads up on CEO. ING angry at GOP brokers - get away."

May 7, 2010 - "Conversation about lease long term vs. short term. CEO very clear; ING executive unable to respond."

June 14-16, 2010 - "CEO long term proposal received. Weak response to proposal; ING Clarion executive clueless about severity of recession. Can't cope with long term correction. Sale of business not imminent; final exit, whenever. What is the $200,000/yr?"

June 24, 2010 - "Meeting to discuss. More info shared. CEO presses for response. Full CEO disclosure, candor."

July 6, 2010 - "NY executive lacks experience; can't deal; recession???? Kick can down the road indefinitely."

ING Clarion delivered a Second Lease Amendment in late June confirming the reluctance to depart from the original rent schedule of early 2007, proposing a quick return to the $50+ per sq. ft. range even as the Park's vacancies were increasing and rents were falling to $40 per sq. ft., or even less. The Second Lease Amendment offered relief for the period August 1 through December 31, 2010.

In November 2010, a representative of Woodland Advisors contacted me and the CEO staff about offices at CEO, primarily at Sound View Drive. Woodland was a firm in occupancy at a Stark facility in Westchester. The rep was seeking an office for a trading group of 4-5 people. He claimed, "I do not like the Stark team, very unresponsive to our needs. We want to move elsewhere."

We went back and forth for several weeks, including evening visits with his team to evaluate space relationships and technology requirements. He obtained considerable information on the space, rental rates, license agreements and CEO's tech infrastructure. In the end, Woodland never responded to our proposal. We learned later that it took space in a new Stark facility in Stamford.

A Third Lease Amendment arrived in early December that extended relief through January 2011. All other provisions and agreements remained in place, especially the $700,000 letter of credit, financial report submissions to Landlord, and prior Confidentiality and Non-Disclosure Agreements.

By mid-January it seemed clear CEO needed to advance its case further. CEO of Greenwich II began paying rent in accordance with its proposal of June 2010, which had received no response.

While CEO was confronting ING Clarion's surprisingly weak response to the recession's impact, the Two Sound View Landlord also remained totally disconnected, apparently preoccupied with other investment distractions.

Intermittent disruptions continued often necessitating a quick response from Loft, Emerge, or both. Pools of water, or other fluids, were a regular sight, especially in the basement garage. A proposal for a short-term rent deferral was received in late September without any mention of building issues.

Then, early Thanksgiving morning, water pipes in the ceilings burst and flooded 14 offices, part of the staff room, and the common area corridors in one section of the first floor. The ensuing pressure changes forced seven HVAC units to explode spewing air conditioning fluid throughout much of the suite.

The disruptions grew and intensified as the building was vacant over the four-day Holiday weekend. Furniture and equipment damages were extensive for CEO and clients. Two clients lost their free-standing data servers to the water and ceiling tiles falling into their offices. Briefcases were ruined by the fluids. Technical devices, soaked in puddles, no longer functioned.

Chaos erupted as clients and staff arrived Monday to see the messy, destructive consequences of building neglect. "This is gross...business interruption! Where's management here?"

While the Landlord's management team had apparently learned of the flooding over the weekend, no one had responded. We rushed in anger to the Landlord's headquarters to demand an immediate management presence on the scene to expedite clean-up, repairs and restoration of the space and offices.

The building failures over the four days of the holiday weekend cost CEO and clients more than $100,000 in immediate out-of-pocket expenses. CEO recovered most of its costs through an insurance claim.

The Landlord cleaned up the mess but was unresponsive to any participation in client cost recoveries. Two clients promptly departed, others were angry, with a few suspending rent payments until their costs were recovered.

The event demonstrated a complete disregard for the lease contract accepted at acquisition in early 2007 and reinforced in the lease renewal in late 2009. The lease detailed specific management and operational requirements for an office building, including a commitment to an atmosphere of "Quiet Enjoyment".

While the record of complaints was extensive, contract essentials had been ignored.

The cumulative evidence, documenting lease contract defaults over four years, was now manifest in the disruptions of the Thanksgiving weekend. I reached out to Attorney Rubin to determine the most appropriate legal response. The building was no longer suitable for the CEO business model.

2011- 2012 Tensions Elevated

The Members Meeting in mid-January focused on the Two Sound View situation, the disruptions, and the Landlord's reactions. The two Members and I meet on a quiet Sunday afternoon for an update and review for the year ahead. Real estate veterans from New York City and Stamford, CT were invited to offer advice regarding responses to the building's situation, the lease and Landlord's role. After some three hours, no new conclusions emerged beyond the fact that a CEO business at Two Sound View was a problem.

CEO II was not mentioned, as the very restrictive Non-Disclosure provisions hampered any open, spontaneous discussions on that subject. QuickBooks year-end financial reports for both CEOs, were given to the two Members.

A couple days later, I received an unexpected call from Yoav Cohen: "Hello Frank, I'm calling to follow up on our meeting last March. My client and I wish to talk more with you about your business and a possible venture together. Are you available for a meeting sometime soon?"

"I'm here in Greenwich every day. Tell me what works for you, although my interest in a sale is no different today than it was last year."

"I understand," he replied. "Let us plan for a meeting in February. I will get back with date and time. Thanks."

While prospective clients cued up for offices at both CEOs, Landlord negotiations progressed very slowly. Dave Rubin was focusing considerable pressure on the Two Sound View Landlord to commit to addressing the office building problems or negotiate some other resolution with its largest and most vulnerable tenant.

In early February, Yoav Cohen called back. "Frank, can we meet on February 16, does that work? Let us say early afternoon."

"No problem Yoav. Where do you want to meet?"

"How about Greenwich Office Park....at... say 1:30?"

"That works, see you then."

The meeting was informal and pleasant. Cohen's client was Adam Stark of Stark Business Solutions, Inc. The firm owned and operated an executive office suite in White Plains and was actively searching for expansion opportunities in Westchester County, NY and Fairfield County, CT. Some informal information was provided, along with brochures.

I organized a comprehensive tour of the suite starting from the large conference room. As we walked through the office areas, it was quickly evident that Stark was already quite familiar with the space. He asked about the acoustical panels adorning the trading room walls. He knew the location of the tech room and what it contained. He favored the 3rd floor terrace overlooking the pond. He knew how to set the controls for the independent HVAC units in each office.

As we concluded, Cohen asked, "We would like to see some financials to further evaluate this opportunity. We wish to send a confidentiality agreement next week to get that process started. Is that OK?"

"Yoav, you may send it, but I wish to repeat I am not looking to sell the business at this time. CEO is not on the market."

A Confidentiality and Non-Disclosure Agreement arrived on

March 4 and was signed by all parties on March 7, 2011. Brief financial details were provided.

In early 2011, ING Group, a Dutch international banking and financial services corporation initiated a divestiture of ING Real Estate Investment Management. ING-REIM consisted of two Clarion entities: Clarion Partners, and Clarion Real Estate Securities.

Clarion Partners was founded in 1982 and developed a significant separate account, real estate investment management program representing institutional investors and pension funds. ING Group acquired Clarion Partners in 1998. Under ING-REIM, Clarion expanded from the separate account private equity market into the public market with real estate funds managed by Clarion Real Estate Securities.

In 2011, Clarion management and a private equity partner acquired Clarion Partners from the ING Group. Soon thereafter, ING Group sold Clarion Real Estate Securities to the publicly traded CBRE Group.

LESSON

Bad Faith, Collusion, Contract Breaches, Tortuous Interference, Violations of Connecticut's Unfair Trade Practices Act

As Clarion's senior management was completing the buyout of the ING Group's ownership interest to become Clarion Partners, LLC, some intermittent communications surfaced involving Clarion and CBRE regarding CEO and Greenwich Office Park, as indicated in the following transcripts from Clarion:

4/4/2011 -"Meeting held. Update, including overture from Stark. GOP not talking to Stark. Repeated assurances." 4/4/2011 -" CEO may need more space, fully rented, Soundview looming. This is analysis paralysis, more info????"

6/1-6/2011 - "Conference call. More analysis. Confirming numbers."

6/13/2011 - "Proposal to CEO drafted. It is high for a suites business. Doesn't leave anything for CEO, acknowledged."

6/29/2011 -"Restates confidentiality requirements - NY executive."

Attorney Rubin was making determined progress with the Two Sound View Landlord. Contract defaults were stressed, and business interference was emphasized. A major rental rate reduction, or a prompt lease termination were on the table.

At the same time, back-and-forth continued with New York office of Clarion, as detailed in the transcripts:

7/5/2011 - "GOP proposal. Take your time. Don't discuss with potential buyers(?). Negotiating in 'good faith'. Confidentiality re-emphasized."

7/11/2011 - "Frank reports another important negotiation. Soundview CEO and landlord."

7/18/2011 - "We need more information."

8/11/2011 - "Executive spills whole story of Kick the Can Down Road - analysis paralysis. Proposed high rent for exec. office suite, no response. Out of element, trying to save job. Sale not imminent ever. Son in background for Frank."

8/11/2011 - "Alerts key broker at CBRE. Frank told to take as much time as needed. Confidential info conveyed to key CBRE broker."

8/16/2011 - "Message to broker: CEO status changed. CEO in play, go for it."

8/31/2011 - "CEO working to close Soundview business."

9/9/2011 - "Message: We are talking to Stark, don't talk to Frank/CEO. Stark rent low, CEO higher. Discussions with Stark and broker meetings."

9/19/2011 - "Message: get more information from Frank for Stark negotiations."

9/20/2011 - "Realized that the Stark deal is less than CEO deal - won't get back to CEO. Big commission exposure now."

9/21/2011 - "Everyone in a quandary, too far along with Stark to get back to CEO. Needs more info from Frank, CEO in play for Stark."

9/27/2011 - "Team meeting. They are pressing for more information on CEO. Accelerating plans to close CEO/Soundview. Confirmed again there were no discussions with Stark, no way. Confidential all the way."

After intense negotiations with the Two Sound View Landlord, a conclusive agreement was achieved in late September. A comprehensive Members meeting was convened in Dave Rubin's office, on October 3, to review the details, benefits, and requirements.

As a result of the weak economy and the well-documented business interference created by the deteriorating physical condition of the building, CEO of Greenwich, LLC would surrender and depart the leased premises by the end of 2011 pursuant to a Settlement Agreement and Release. The Agreement released CEO from some $3 million in future rent obligations.

Meanwhile, the Clarion/CBRE team had gotten a quick update:

9/30/2011 - "Soundview closing accelerates."

10/19/2011 - "More data requested; no mention of proposal or anything about lease negotiations. Express enthusiasm for CEO client moves to GOP."

10/31/2011 - "CEO/Soundview closing goes public. Clients start planning moves to GOP, may need more space. Furniture, tech issues addressed on a daily basis."

11/17/2011 - "David Rubin letter reiterating June 2010 proposal gets no response."

11/30/2011 - "Landlord's commission exposure is calculated at $663,840. Whole CEO L/C would go to pay a completely unnecessary commission."

The prior ING Clarion team had changed the GOP management and leasing structure in 2008. A Clarion/CBRE property management and leasing team was established on site, with exclusive control of all brokerage operations for the Park. That turn of events represented a potential revenue windfall for CBRE as it offered the prospect of commission revenue on some 400,000 sq. ft. of office space, in addition to management fees.

As a practical matter, these management and operational changes seemed to eliminate any possible barrier (a/k/a "Chinese wall") between the Clarion/CBRE fiduciary, client relationship with the Oregon state pension fund ownership, and the Clarion/CBRE brokerage focus on transactions and fees.

CBRE was fundamentally a commercial brokerage business driven by real estate commissions. Everyone, including property management personnel, would be incentivized to deliver lucrative commissions through various participation or referral arrangements. The brokers and agents were all independent contractors.

The availability of leasing commissions became especially intense in the post-2008 period as new leasing plunged, vacancies mounted, and commission fees all but evaporated. Commercial brokers began prospecting everywhere for leasing commission opportunities. At GOP, the CBRE team was especially protective of its exclusive territory, and interlopers were aggressively thwarted. Any new leases, renegotiations or renewals would be handled by CBRE, without exception.

It was in this environment that key brokers at CBRE were provided regular "status" reports on worrisome tenancies, renegotiations, and renewals. CEO would have been in these status communications as one of the largest tenants in the Park. Because of its size (14,752 sq. ft.), it also prompted regular inquiry from senior brokers, and unannounced visits to the suite. Management responses appeared to have been cautionary; "don't do anything, yet!"

But in August of 2011, as CEO was meeting and talking with Clarion/CBRE on a "confidential basis" about everything, including the CEO/Sound View closing, a message was sent to a key CBRE broker, "the CEO status has changed -- CEO is in play." Management appeared to move aggressively to obtain financials and projections to facilitate the GOP/Stark discussions.

At the same time, they encouraged and facilitated the substantial relocation of CEO clients from Two Sound View Drive to GOP to bolster the business of CEO of Greenwich II, LLC, which they had now "put in play" through the CBRE broker.

In January 2012, mail arrived at Suite 300 for Stark Office Suites of Greenwich LLC. Verizon sent Stark Office Suites "Congratulations on your new business". Paychex payroll confirmation forms arrived for Stark Office Suites in early February. A quick inquiry through CT.gov revealed Stark Office Suites of Greenwich LLC was a newly registered Connecticut business at 2 Greenwich Office Park, 3rd Floor, Greenwich, CT 06831.

In April, the Landlord abruptly declared CEO of Greenwich II, LLC (the Tenant) in default, and promptly terminated the lease without any constructive response to two years of overtures, or the comprehensive proposal presented in June 2010. The Landlord wanted rents in the $50 to $55 per sq. ft. range, pre-recession rates. In May, Landlord drew down on the letter of credit in the amount of $483,353.89.

I quickly called Attorney Rubin. "Dave, how do I respond to this? The Landlord has avoided or rebuffed every overture from me. What can we do now?"

"Frank, I don't know what's driving their behavior. As you know, the market is very weak, but you have a good, credible following at CEO. I don't understand their complete failure to respond."

I then asked, "Is this behavior coming from the Oregon pension fund, or is it Clarion and CBRE?"

"I wish I could answer that question, Frank. The only people we are dealing with are Clarion, CBRE and their lawyers in Stamford."

After a moment he said, "The only action we can take right now is to appeal the 'motion to quit'. If the court accepts our appeal, we might have time to facilitate either a resolution or a relocation. You have a well-established business that you don't want to give up."

"Well, there's no doubt about that Dave. I have been getting inquiries from other owner/operators in this changing workspace format, one from Westchester, one from New Jersey and one from Florida. This concept is taking off," I replied.

Dave continued, "I believe we can establish 'bad faith' immediately. Given the lengthy interval, the number of individual participants, the number of meetings and a comprehensive proposal that got no reply whatsoever, I believe we could also advance other legal elements to reinforce the appeal."

After a pause, he added, "New meetings with the Landlord's representatives, and its legal counsel, could also provide new insights. But this will take time, cost money, and will be a big distraction from the business itself. Understood?"

"Yes, Dave, thanks. I appreciate your advice and help."

Confrontation. CEO of Greenwich II, LLC., through Attorney Rubin, appealed the lease termination in Superior Court. The following summarizes Attorney Rubin's submission to the Court:

- "Clarion Partners, LLC is the real estate investment manager for the Ownership/Landlord responsible for the operation, management and leasing of Greenwich Office Park (GOP), including Building 2.
- "CBRE, Inc. was engaged by Clarion, on behalf of ownership, to oversee the management and leasing of Greenwich Office Park and Building 2, reporting to Clarion Partners.
- "Based on all information and evidence, no "Chinese Wall" existed separating Clarion Partners, the CBRE management division, and the CBRE brokerage/leasing division to prevent the utilization of confidential information relating to a GOP tenant for the benefit of CBRE and its brokers.
- "CEO of Greenwich II, LLC, the Tenant, collateralized the subject lease in 2007 with a Letter of Credit in the amount of $800,000 which was subsequently reduced to $700,000.
- "In September 2008, Lehman Brothers went bankrupt, and the ensuing events drove the country into the "Great Recession".
- "As a result, beginning in the fourth quarter of 2008, the fair rental value for office space in GOP abruptly declined. Soon thereafter, vacancies dramatically increased, and rents fell further.

- "In January 2009, Tenant first approached Clarion and CBRE management about rent relief. In September 2009, Landlord and Tenant entered into a First Lease Amendment, deferring rent to be paid by Tenant for the period March 1, 2009 through May 31, 2010. Clarion and CBRE negotiated the rent relief and presented the Amendment as a "take it or leave it" offer."
- "For more than three years from 2009 through most of 2012, Tenant sought, through Clarion and CBRE, to negotiate a long-term solution to permit the business to remain in GOP over the Lease term in a format consistent with the business model and the overall economic environment.
- "Over the three-year period, Clarion and CBRE, in various ways, led Tenant to believe something could be worked out to reflect actual market and business conditions. Tenant continued to press for a long-term relief arrangement.
- "In August 2010, Landlord's agents presented another "take it or leave it proposition" providing limited rent relief through December 2010 in a Second Amendment to the Lease.
- "Again, in December 2010, Tenant was provided another "take it or leave it proposition" providing limited rent relief through January 2011 in the Third Lease Amendment.
- "As part of these Lease Amendment negotiations, Tenant agreed to provide Landlord, through Clarion and CBRE, with monthly and annual confidential and proprietary financial information and documentation relating to its business. These reports included monthly and annual profit and loss statements, cash flow projections, client lists and annual balance sheets.
- "As a result, Landlord and its agents were fully informed regarding all aspects of Tenant's business, services and clients.
- "Because of the nature of the confidential and proprietary business and financial information to be provided, in February 2009, in connection with the negotiation and execution of the First Lease Amendment, Landlord and Tenant entered into a Confidentiality Agreement entitled a Non-Disclosure Agreement in which Landlord and its agents agreed that "it will not use, reveal or divulge any aspect of the Confidential Renegotiation without the specific, prior written consent of Tenant." Confidentiality was a priority of the Landlord and Tenant from inception of negotiations. A similar Agreement was included in the Lease in March 2007.
- "The Non-Disclosure Agreement protected Tenant from improper and surreptitious dissemination of Tenant's confidential business information to competitors or the larger Greenwich business community. In addition, the Agreement protected Tenant from the disclosure of the existence of Lease re-negotiations, since such disclosure could jeopardize business, client relationships, and its reputation in the business community.
- "Tenant relied on the representations and warrantees of the Landlord and its agents in the Non-Disclosure Agreement. Tenant has since learned that it disseminated such confidential business and financial

information to its severe detriment.

- "Clarion and CBRE, Landlord's agents throughout, were bound by the obligations under the Non-Disclosure Agreement.
- "Beginning in 2009 through 2012, the Landlord, through Clarion and CBRE, breached the Non-Disclosure Agreement by disseminating to all that Tenant was distressed under the traumatic recessionary shocks, and sought to engage the Landlord to renegotiate the Lease.
- "In June 2010, Tenant proposed to the Landlord, through its agents, a revision to the Lease Agreement that reset the rent schedule to reflect current economic and market conditions and provide for the recovery of deferred rent over time. It had become clear that Tenant could not maintain its tenancy under the rent schedule of the 2007 Lease due to the extremely weak market conditions and the economic distress affecting clients. Tenant stressed that in order to remain a viable entity the pre-recession Lease had to be restructured to the current norms.
- "After the expiration of the Third Amendment, Tenant began paying rent consistent with its June 2010 proposed revision to the Lease Agreement, which payments the Landlord accepted.
- "Tenant continued to make rent payments consistent with the proposal and submit to Landlord and its agents its proprietary and confidential business reports through March 2012, without any written response or counter proposal to Tenant's proposal advanced in June 2010.
- "The 2007 Lease contains a non-compete clause whereby Landlord agreed that, during the term of the Lease, Landlord will not lease or provide office space in Greenwich Office Park to any tenant whose primary purpose is to operate an executive office suite, shared office space, or any similar temporary office space business in the Park. This provision was an essential contractual element of the Lease, relied upon by the Tenant.
- "A regional competitor in the executive office suite business is Stark Office Suites, a company with established installations in New York City, Westchester County, and Stamford, CT. By all accounts Stark was exploring expansion opportunities in Fairfield County and Greenwich, CT.
- "Landlord was prohibited from leasing to Stark at Greenwich Office Park due to the non-compete provision of the Tenant's Lease.
- "During mid-2011, in several meetings with Tenant, Clarion stated and represented to Tenant's Managing Member that it did not, and would not, engage in discussions with Stark relating to Tenant or the leasing of premises to Stark. It affirmed that it wanted to work with Tenant to restructure the Lease. Tenant relied on these statements.
- "In August 2011, Landlord through its agents Clarion and CBRE began secret negotiations with Stark to lease the Tenant's premises to Stark.
- "In the Fourth Quarter of 2011, the Members of CEO of Greenwich, LLC (a separate entity with the same Members and Membership structure) announced the termination of its lease at Two Sound View Drive in Greenwich, CT. The 16,106 sq. ft. installation provided 54 fur-

nished offices to the CEO business at Two Sound View Drive.

- "In September and October 2011 Tenant informed Landlord and its agents that many clients   (licensees) from Sound View were relocating to GOP and entering new license agreements for offices in the CEO of Greenwich II premises at GOP.
- "Landlord and its agents encouraged and supported the relocation of these clients to GOP at the very time it was secretly negotiating with Stark to lease the premises out from under Tenant.
- "Many such licensees relocated their businesses to GOP. The Landlord and its agents knew this relocation process was expensive for Tenant, as it involved the transfer of technology and phone systems, computers, client amenities, furniture, and related items to Tenant's premises.
- "Landlord and its agents approved, encouraged, and supported this transition to GOP, the growth, profitability, and revenue stream it represented, all the while accepting the rent tendered consistent Tenant's proposed Lease revision.
- "Implicit in the behavior of Landlord and its agents was the sense that Landlord was not seeking to terminate Tenant's Lease without further negotiations. CBRE, in fact, inquired whether Tenant wished to lease additional space to accommodate the demand.
- "By negotiating directly with Stark and Stark's real estate broker, beginning in August 2011, Landlord and its agents breached the Non-Disclosure Agreement by disclosing and disseminating to a direct competitor, and the brokers, the status of Tenant at GOP and its efforts to restructure the Lease.
- "In late September 2011, Landlord and its agents received an offer from Stark to lease Tenant's premises. Upon receipt of the offer, Clarion began to evaluate Stark's offer with Tenant's June 2010 proposal to restructure the existing lease.
- "In the process, Clarion began requesting more confidential financial information, ostensibly to revisit Tenant's June proposal but, in fact, to evaluate the Stark proposal with Tenant's proprietary information, in direct violation of the Non-Disclosure Agreement and Connecticut common law. Tenant provided all requested information and documentation through January 2012.
- "Unbeknownst to Tenant, Landlord and its agents continued to negotiate with Stark, and in February 2012 a term sheet was entered into between the Landlord and Stark for the premises.
- "During the negotiation between the Landlord and its agents, and Stark and its agents, the Landlord and its agents expressly negotiated providing Stark with Tenant's infrastructure and assets for the operation of an executive office suite business. These provisions were fundamental to the negotiations between the Landlord and Stark.
- "The resulting term sheet between the Landlord and Stark included the Landlord and its agents providing Stark with Tenant's infrastructure and assets for the executive office suite business.
- "As of April 2012, as a result of the influx of clients from the business at Two Sound View Drive Tenant's occupancy rate approached

100%. Furthermore, all infrastructure was in place for profitable, fully furnished, and modern office suite business, including, without limitation, leasehold improvements valued at $270,000, computer, phone and technology equipment valued at $120,000, and furniture and fixtures valued at approximately $300,000. Tenant's premises were fully equipped to operate the executive office suite business for the remainder of the Lease term.

- "Notwithstanding the well-documented record of Tenant's three years of quiet, good-faith negotiations and a proposal, complete and timely disclosure of proprietary confidential information, a Landlord supported relocation of clients and infrastructure from Two Sound View Drive, and the existence of a $700,000 Letter of Credit securing the Lease, Landlord and its agents entered into an agreement with Stark Office Suites for the purpose of leasing Tenant's premises to Stark, appropriating Tenant's business and providing Stark with a fully functional office suite business, all in violation of the Lease contract, the Non-Disclosure Agreement, and Connecticut common law and Statute Section 42-110b regarding Unfair Trade Practices.

- "On or about April 10, 2012, as Tenant was paying rent to Landlord and reconfiguring offices for newly arrived clients, Stark formed a new business entity and filed documents with the Connecticut Secretary of State reflecting the formation of a business entity named Stark Office Suites of Greenwich, LLC.

- "Soon thereafter, the Landlord abruptly declared the Tenant in default, and promptly terminated the Lease with a Notice to Quit.

- "On approximately May 29, 2012, having strung Tenant along for over a three-year period, Landlord drew on the Letter of Credit in the amount of $483,353.89, reflecting deferred rent and rent shortfall from Tenant under the Lease for the three-year period."

The Court accepted the appeal. In response, the Court required an independent assessment of current commercial office rent levels. Kerin Associates, a commercial real estate appraisal firm, was accepted by the Court and retained to document market conditions and recommend a market-based "use-and-occupancy" rent level for Suite 300 during the appeal process.

Based on a full market analysis and supporting data, the Kerin recommendation was $35 per sq. ft., which the court accepted as the market rate.

At this almost three-year anniversary of the Greenwich Office Park silence, Corporate Executive Offices decided to take a proactive stance with respect the future of its business, and the evolving business model in this new era.

CEO would now pay a "use and occupancy" rent to the Court as litigation and negotiations progressed. Soon CEO was suing the Landlord for "bad faith" negotiations, tortuous interference with Tenant's business, breach of strict confidentiality agreements, collusion with competitors, and other Unfair Trade Practices to force a forfeiture. Counsel advised that this process could take many months even years, during which time CEO would be paying the "use and occupancy" cost.

For some reason, Clarion and CBRE seemed to think the recession had little impact on the CEO business at the beginning of discussions. The Landlord and its representatives saw high occupancy and quality clientele at CEO throughout the lease term, even in the stressful 2009-2010 period. In 2012, a surge in activity occurred as a large percentage of loyal clients relocated from Two Sound View.

The fact that Corporate Executive Offices was among the best performing executive office suite, shared offices businesses in Fairfield County did not mean that CEO skirted the recession. The 2012 rental rates were at pre-2006 levels. As in many sectors of the economy, a 25-30% price reset had occurred. The CEO business was no exception. Yet it responded to these wrenching economic events, sudden demographic shifts and rapid technological changes with focused commitment and continuity, in order to make a positive difference for clients and others in the area's business community.

In the larger Greenwich and Fairfield County office markets, the experiences were alarmingly negative, and the outlook rather grim. Vacancies rose and rental rates fell. Long term tenants had closed or departed for less expensive locations. The events produced increased office vacancies, weak demand, and a dramatic decline in commission revenue, especially at Greenwich Office Park.

Nevertheless, Landlord's representatives entered secretive, separate discussions with a competitor from another locale. Its chief executive and other cohorts made unannounced off-hours visits to the CEO premises to gather data, make observations, and take quick photos. It seemed these explorations started in 2010. This firm was represented in the market by a well-known CBRE broker.

Now CEO was in Norwalk Housing Court to pursue direct actions against the Landlord. It soon became clear the Landlord was concerned about many of these allegations, particularly those asserting violations of Connecticut's Unfair Trade Practices Act (CUTPA). All were supported by documents and the testimony reported from numerous depositions.

During the protracted trial process, interrupted by the death of Judge Hauser after the trial had commenced, Landlord and Tenant continued to negotiate a resolution that would enable CEO to remain a viable business entity in Greenwich Office Park. These discussions continued into early 2013.

Members Informed. Soon after the "Default Notice" was issued in April 2012, and in the months thereafter, a series of Members Meetings were conducted in Attorney Rubin's offices in Stamford, in the interest of full disclosure. The two active Members focused on financial liabilities and consequences.

Dave Rubin emphasized that the Managing Member was the guarantor and would be responsible for that element of any outcome. It would be resolved between McBrearity and First County Bank. The two Members were invited to contact Rubin at any time with questions or concerns, to observe discussions with Landlord's counsel, and to attend proceedings or hearings in the Norwalk Housing Court. Neither responded to any of the invitations to be a part of the process.

Resolution. After months of intermittent Court appearances, and many weeks of meetings with Dave Rubin and Landlord's counsel, a negotiated settlement was reached in the first quarter of 2013. In March 2013, the Landlord and Tenant, CEO of Greenwich Il, LLC, entered a Stipulation before the Housing Court, and a Settlement Agreement, both signed by the Managing Member in his corporate capacity, and individually as guarantor.

The CEO business had to vacate by September 30, 2013, without any further recourse, leaving the 3rd floor suite in "broom-clean" condition. Pursuant to the Agreements, Landlord drew down the balance remaining on the Letter of Credit ($216,646.11) and released CEO of Greenwich II, LLC, and the Managing Member from all other obligations under the lease.

It had been clear for some months that CEO would be in a new transition phase. As 2012 was entering its final quarter, the business was 90% rented and very stable. With a large base of busy, new-generation office clients, and a growing roster of "virtual" clients, a fresh venue had to be found. The backlog of inquiries suggested another 10-15 offices could be rented. It seemed essential to reestablish the now vibrant business in a stable, long-term situation. I had reached out to our broker in September for an evaluation of available options for this new direction. Selected visits and broker meetings had already occurred.

Soon after our annual Super Bowl party in New Canaan, I met with a Member at a local coffee shop in New Canaan for an update on CEO matters, the final Stipulation in Housing Court, and the Settlement Agreement. He soon asked, "What are your plans going forward?"

I told him, "I'll be trying to do another. It is a good business, with a strong following, killed largely by the recession. And I owe a lot of money."

He looked at me for a few moments, then said, "Other Members won't like it. You should know one Member is likely to get seriously angry." The conversation ended on that note.

Soon after, as I was contemplating a new location and accommodating new client arrivals, I got a surprising message from our broker. "Frank, that suspicious, gossipy broker is at it again, claiming to be prospecting for deals. He contacted me today to find out what I might be looking for in the market. He really wants to know what I might be doing for you if anything. I told him I didn't have any news, all is quiet."

I paused in disbelief. "The former Member's 'gossip guy', is at it again. I cannot believe it. What did I do to prompt such behavior? These were once good friends that I had deferred to, to my detriment. Now at least one is still after me."

On Tuesday April 30, I got a message from the angry Member. "Frank, I would like to meet with you this week......just to re-connect and hopefully move forward on any new business situation."

I promptly replied: "As I discussed with another Member earlier, I am moving ahead in a new format with a new entity. I appreciate your inquiry, but under the post-recession circumstances, I need to start afresh. Best wishes."

The review of availabilities had begun in late 2012. Our broker had concluded: "The best opportunity to do this is right across West Putnam Avenue at 75 Holly Hill Lane. New owners have a largely vacant building acquired out of foreclosure. It is unique, formerly known as 'The Greenwich Atrium'. They are planning a major renovation to bring the building current with architectural refinements, current technologies, and extensive modernization of public spaces. It has a large multi-level garage with entries on multiple levels. A big work-letter is offered."

"An 'atrium' building, garage parking, right nearby, this appears to be a uniquely attractive opportunity, with perfect timing. I am still responding to numerous investor and operator inquiries. Maybe this is the place to be."

"I think so. The new Holly Hill ownership is eager to secure a large tenant known to the Greenwich market. They are offering competitive rates and terms, including a generous free rent period after lease commencement. I think you may be able to pick the space in the building that works best for you and your clients. We should engage the ownership very soon. This could be it."

"Absolutely, let's get it on the calendar, and move ahead."

The Atrium at 75 Holly Hill Lane, 2013
CEO Moving On

6. LESSONS - ARBITRATION 2014-2016

The Confrontation

As we were completing the final aspects of our relocation to 75 Holly Hill Lane in late 2013, I got a call from Attorney Rubin. "Frank, I just got a call from a lawyer representing your Members. Apparently, they believe they have a claim or dispute with you regarding the business affairs of the CEO LLCs."

"Dave, who is the lawyer? Do you know him?"

"I don't know him, and never heard of him. He is a lawyer licensed in Rhode Island. His name is Timothy Cohane."

"What, what's the name again? Cocaine?" I asked.

"His name is Co....Hane, h...a...n... e." He replied.

"Is the legal world 'high' on him? Are the Members 'high' on him?"

"Frank, this is not a moment for wordplay. He is not licensed in Connecticut. I do not know how the Members would know him. That's all I know."

"Well, what is the claim or dispute? You've hosted most of the recent Members Meetings, what could be at issue, at this time?"

"I don't have any details yet," Dave replied. "Cohane asserts they are responding to Article X, the Arbitration provision, in the LLC Operating Agreements. This is standard 'boilerplate' in such documents. Since I do not have these agreements, I will need to get copies to review before I respond further. Please get me copies."

"Will do. Steve Steinmetz prepared them. I'll get fresh copies of the final documents from Steve and e-mail them to you." The following morning, I responded. "Dave, I sent you the Agreements."

"Okay Frank, thanks. Let me review the documents and talk further with Cohane. I know all the details of the CEO Sound View situation and CEO II at GOP. I hosted some of your meetings. You are the guarantor with a serious debt obligation. They had good distributions, special tax benefits, and full disclosure throughout. I do not know what the issues could be. But I will report soon, and Happy New Year."

A formal letter was sent by Attorney Timothy Cohane to David Rubin on January 18, 2014:

"As agreed in our phone conversation I am attaching a list of information which my clients and I need to determine whether mediation is called for under the Arbitration provision. There have been numerous, documented attempts by my clients to receive information without good results. A response to this request that information was previously provided will not satisfy this request for information. We have searched the files previously provided and are missing the information we now request.

In the event that this request is not fully met by February 15, 2014 we will assume that Mr. McBrearity is unwilling to mediate. We will then proceed to a Court jurisdiction."

Upon a quick review, I called Dave. "The attorney's letter of January 18, 2014 has an attachment detailing an information request. This attachment was not prepared or proofed by the attorney as many typographical, grammatical, and technical errors are evident throughout. The writer clearly had no access to the substantial files of information already provided in late last year and in earlier intervals. All the requested information is provided in the three boxes of files.

"Other information was also provided in various meetings and e-mail exchanges in the 2010 – 2013 period. Certain items, particularly items 6 – 10, reflect input from an outsider with commercial real estate knowledge, but little knowledge of CEO or the executive suite industry. The following phrases stand out: tenants, leases, vacancies, among others.

"It was long-ago explained to the Members that the CEO business rents offices under license agreements or 'services agreements' to CEO's renters or clients. The only lease that exists is between Tenant (CEO) and the Landlord. Frequent use of the words, leases, tenants, etc. reflects input from an uninformed outsider.

"And how did they know 'CEO Holly Hill' specifically, except through a local broker source? I strongly suspect that a Member's broker friend had a large role in the preparation of this list. He has already been searching around, making inquiries.

"The writer lacks access to e-mails and other communications in 2012. All services agreements had expired in 2013, as CEO II was closing. CEO II was unable to legitimately enter into any new services agreements in that period.

"Moreover, the substantial leasehold improvements and fixed assets had become the Landlord's property and could not be removed and relocated when CEO II closed.

"In late 2011 or early 2012, as we were closing CEO at Sound View and moving clients to CEO II, we were preparing income tax returns for 2011. I asked the Members if they wanted formal year-end financials for 2011 for both CEOs. The answer was NO!!... not worth the expense.

"I fail to understand how this information request is relevant, or in any way consistent with the LLC Operating Agreement as to the following: Article VI Management, Paragraphs 6.3 and 6.4; Article VIII Dissolution, Paragraphs 8.1 and 8.2.; and Article XI General Provisions, Paragraph 11.1."

After a pause Dave asked, "Is this broker source the same person who prompted the 'gossip guys' assertions from Greenwich Office Park?"

"I am certain it is." I replied.

Since I did not know anything about this Arbitration provision I had agreed to, it was now time to check it in the two 21-page Operating Agreements:

10.1 Arbitration. In the event that there arise any claims or disputes regarding the construction, performance, validity or enforceability of this Agreement, or the rights and obligations of the parties to this Agreement in connection with the business affairs of the Company, then the parties thereto agree to submit to matter to non-binding mediation. If such mediation is unsuccessful, then the parties shall submit their dispute to binding arbitration in accordance with the rules of the American Arbitration Association. The decision of such arbitrator shall be final and binding on the parties. The arbitrator may grant any remedy or relief, including, but not limited to, specific performance of a contract or contractual right and equitable or injunctive relief, and attorneys fees. The forum for such arbitration shall be Fairfield County, Connecticut. Resolution by mediation and arbitration shall be determined persuant to the laws of the State of Connecticut, both as to procedure and substance. Arbitration shall be the sole and exclusive remedy as regards any such dispute and a final judgment of a court of competent jurisdiction may be entered upon the arbitrator's award.

It certainly was "boilerplate." It even had typos. I wondered if an arbitration specialist was needed to address these potential claims. Dave Rubin certainly knew what and how events and relationships played out in the recession's tumult. I wondered if Attorney Cohane was a specialist in the arbitration format. I went to the internet to learn more about Tim Cohane.

According to Wikipedia, Timothy Cohane was a highly decorated Vietnam war veteran, college basketball coach, Wall Street trader, and now a sports lawyer. Cohane spent most of his post-war career coaching basketball. After a five-year stint at Dartmouth in the early 1980s, he ventured into securities trading.

In 1993, he was hired as head basketball coach at the University of Buffalo. He resigned at the beginning of the 1999-2000 season, as a result of an investigation in which he was alleged to have violated NCAA rules.

I was surprised at this revelation from the published records. A friend of my daughter was engaged to a young man who aspired to be a basketball coach after college. It was 1999, and he was recruited by several schools in the northeast, reasonably close to families and friends. He had accepted an offer to be an assistant at the University of Buffalo. But when he arrived, he discovered the head coach was gone. The young man quickly recovered to find a favorable coaching position at a southern school.

After his resignation, Cohane filed lawsuits, first against the University of Buffalo, then against both the University and the NCAA accusing them of conspiring to remove him as coach. In the interim, Cohane studied at the University of Rhode Island and the Roger Williams University School of Law to obtain a law degree and leverage off his experiences in collegiate sports. As he awaited the resolution of his long-running appeal, he developed a law practice specializing in due-process protections to coaches and student-athletes, "Tim Cohane Sports Law."

I called Dave Rubin. "Dave, how would this 'sports lawyer' know the Members?"

"Frank, I wish I had answers here. He is pushing this 'boilerplate' clause to get a settlement or get some fees. That is all I know. They are asserting an unspecified claim or dispute. This is how it gets handled, per the agreement."

"Dave, based on what I just read, he could push this for a long time."

"Frank, we have to take one thing at a time. The agreement commits you to a non-binding mediation. After that, an arbitration if necessary. The American Arbitration Association requires everything to be confidential. Right now, Cohane and I need to agree on a mediator. I will keep you posted. Take care."

A very comprehensive three-page Confidentiality and Non-Disclosure Agreement was issued and signed by the two Claimants and the Respondent in early February. The document strongly emphasized the confidentiality of this process.

"The Claimants agree that it would be impossible or inadequate to measure and calculate the damages from any breach of the covenants set forth in this Agreement. Accordingly, the Claimants agree that if either of them breaches or threatens to breach this Agreement, Respondent will have available, in addition to any other right or remedy available, including monetary damages and/or claims of breach of fiduciary duty under the respective Operating Agreements, the right to obtain an injunction from a court of competent jurisdiction restraining such breach or threatened breach and to specific performance of any such provision of this Agreement." Signed by Respondent on February 7, 2014.

The Assertions

After several communications between Rubin and Cohane, a March 17 letter to Dave Rubin summarized the threatening issues Cohane was retained to address on behalf of the Members, as follows:

"As discussed in our meeting at your office on March 11, 2014, the Members have asked me to work with you to seek a resolution to issues involving Frank B. McBrearity, Jr. for his acts and omissions as Managing Member of CEO I, CEO II, and CEO Holly Hill ("the companies"). The documentation indicate that McBrearity may have breached his duties under Connecticut Law.

"As reiterated, the Members have repeatedly been denied access to an explanation as to all things affecting member's rights. I am enclosing a partial list of activity by McBrearity which indicate potential claims against McBrearity of: Breach of Contract, Negligence, Breach of Covenant of Good Faith and Fair Dealing, Breach of Fiduciary Duties, Statutory Theft, Conversion, Equitable Accounting, Violation of Connecticut's Unfair Trade Practices Act and Defamation Slander and Defamation Libel.

"Please send us the information we requested in our January 6, 2014 phone call, and follow-up letter so we can move ahead with the mediation component. In the absence of the requested information, we are in the process of preparing a complaint and a move toward litigation. I am available to come again and meet at your office between April 7 and April !8."

I had to call Dave. "Dave I am the guarantor of the financing, at their insistence. Plus, they got distributions, tax benefits and full disclosure. What is going on?"

"Frank, someone is angry, but this is really off. I don't have an answer."

The Mediation

After additional meetings, an agreement was reached in late April on a qualified mediator. The chosen attorney was James T. (Tim) Shearin, a lawyer with Pullman & Comley in Stamford, CT. A mediation session was scheduled for May 27, 2014 at Attorney Shearin's office in Stamford.

On May 21, in advance of this meeting, Attorney Rubin set forth our position on this surprising confrontation with two of the LLCs' Members, as follows:

"This matter is being pursued by two Members of the two CEO LLCs, the 'Claimants'. A third Member had chosen not to participate in this matter.

"At the outset, we must stress this is an unusual mediation in that there is no pending action to describe and identify what is being mediated. We are unsure as to what is actually at issue. Our understanding is that the Claimants are using the mediation process to obtain information and documentation, while generally alluding to improper transactions by McBrearity as Managing Member of the LLCs. The Claimants have failed to identify any possible measure of damages for their alleged grievances.

"We must cite three key provisions in the Operating Agreements of the two LLCs:

- 'Article VI, Management: Rights Powers and Duties. Under this Article, McBrearity, as Manager, has full, exclusive, and complete discretion to manage, control, administer and operate the business and affairs of the company.
- 'Article VIII, Dissolution. The company shall be dissolved upon the loss of premises. Further, upon dissolution, on winding up the company, the assets shall be distributed first to the creditors of the company.

- 'Article XI, General Provisions. The Manager shall not be liable, responsible or accountable in damages or otherwise to any member of the company for any act performed within the scope of the authority conferred by this agreement except for fraud, gross negligence, or an intentional breach of the Agreement.'

"From a documentation and information standpoint, McBrearity has provided Claimants with every record of the business activities of the two CEOs since inception. Members were provided boxes of documents relating to both CEOs. Subsequent to Attorney Cohane's request for information, we extracted all of the CEOs QuickBooks financial files onto a flash drive for full transmission of the CEO's entire financial history to the Claimants.

"We have provided, in multiple formats, all financing and transactional documentation relating to CEO's bank loans for which McBrearity, as the Managing Member of the dissolved LLCs, is the guarantor and personally responsible for debt in the amount of $900,000. Berkow, Schechter & Co., CPA accountants for the LLCs, has provided the Claimants with responsive accounting records and information, with directions to contact them with any questions. No document or financial record has been withheld from the Claimants at any time.

"The Claimants appear to be threatening to sue McBrearity for breach of fiduciary duty, and other similar torts, in connection with the disbursement and accounting of LLC money in McBrearity's capacity as Managing Member of the LLCs.

"However, the Claimants appear to be seeking payment of money directly to them in their individual capacities as Members when, by law, any such claims, if they did exist, should be brought as a derivative action on behalf of the LLC entities.

"Moreover, assuming, for arguments sake, that such claims did exist derivatively, any funds owed would be paid by McBrearity directly to the LLCs to be used to satisfy the outstanding debt which McBrearity has guaranteed and is currently paying personally. Additionally, McBrearity would have a claim against the LLCs for indemnification for the recovery of the funds he has been paying to the LLCs' banks, as guarantor, for years. Therefore, the Claimants have not sustained and cannot evidence any damages whatsoever, regardless of how the claims are brought, or the merits of the allegations, which are strongly disputed.

"Finally, it is worth noting that the entirety of the Claimants capital contributions to the LLCs is less than $200,000 each. Furthermore, prior to the economic collapse of 2008, the Claimants routinely received distributions of approximately $15,000 per quarter, along with extensive income tax deductions resulting from large annual depreciation amounts from the fixed asset accounts in the corporate balance sheets.

"In short, the net losses to the Claimants from their investments in the two CEO LLCs are minimal, if any. In contrast, McBrearity's liability as guarantor of the LLCs debt totals $900,000 and is secured by his home.

"In summary, this is simply a situation where a real estate-based investment went south due to the 'bursting' of the real estate bubble and the most significant downturn in the economy since the Great Depression. The Managing Member, who was under tremendous pressure over several years, with great personal exposure and liability, did all he could under the circumstances to preserve and protect the interests of the LLC entities and the Members, while personally paying a price for the confluence of events that effected millions. The Claimants, having no personal exposure and having recouped most, if not all, of their investments, have no sustainable grounds for their grievances."

Attorney Shearin's mediation session on May 27 reviewed Attorney Rubin's presentation, and sought to explore Claimants' assertions as to what was to be mediated. The Mediator probed the Members for specific claims and disputes. The Claimants offered brief comments, but few specifics. Dave Rubin and I soon departed, leaving the mediation to Shearin, Cohane, and the Members.

In late June, Tim Shearin, as mediator, responded with his conclusions. He thought Claimants' assertions should be addressed as derivative actions through the LLC entities, and not as a direct action against the Managing Member. In addition, based on the mediation, he believed such an action would not succeed.

Dave and I met at his office on September 22 for an update. "Frank, I continue to hear from Cohane. They are planning to file a Demand for Arbitration with the American Arbitration Association."

"Dave, given the Mediator's conclusions, do we have to respond to this?"

"If you don't respond to the Arbitration, the arbitrator, selected by them, simply will hear the Members' case and render a decision based on their unimpeached and uncontroverted testimony and documentation. Their attorney then will file a Motion to Confirm the arbitration award in the Connecticut Superior Court, which will be granted absent objection. Unfortunately, you have little choice but to defend yourself in the arbitration."

"But Dave, the Mediator's conclusions were rather specific and direct."

"Yes, for sure. But the mediator is not an arbitrator. His thoughts have no bearing on the arbitration. Further, the arbitrator may not agree."

"Damn Dave, we don't even know what is really in dispute."

"Very true, Frank, but the requirements for filing a Demand for Arbitration, unfortunately, permit a very brief and generic description of any claim. What we do know, at this time, is that they have only brought individual actions by the Members against you as fiduciary. They have not brought a derivative action on behalf of the LLC entities which, in my view, is the proper way to stylize this action. We need to be cautious. They could amend their Demand."

"Do you really think Cohane knows what a 'derivative action' is? If he really knew what he was doing it should have been brought up much earlier."

"Frank, I can't answer that. He is not a veteran lawyer. That's all I can say."

"Well, if we must respond, is there a way I can recover legal fees, time and travel expenses, and related costs if we succeed with our defense?"

"Yes, possibly. The Operating Agreement permits an arbitrator to award attorneys' fees in connection with any arbitration. It does not mandate it. It is completely up to the discretion of the arbitrator. The recovery of those costs is dependent on it being awarded by the arbitrator. Connecticut law does not permit the successful party in an arbitration to sue for vexatious litigation."

"Dave, how did I get into this? I've been fighting the 'Great Recession', now this."

"All I can say is that it's a boilerplate provision in such agreements, in a tactic to keep some disputes out of the court system. Also, you do not have to be a Connecticut-registered lawyer to push arbitration. And you signed off on it."

"What's in dispute?"

"We'll have to wait and find out."

Dave called the morning of December 9. "Frank, I am having a conference call today with Tim Cohane about the arbitration. He said the call will include Stewart I. Edelstein, an attorney with Cohen and Wolf, and a veteran arbitrator, and a Karen Jalkut of the American Arbitration Association. I know Stew Edelstein. He is a well-regarded attorney and arbitrator: experienced, competent, professional."

"Do you need me on the call?"

"No, this is a preliminary hearing with them to confirm the provisions of the Operating Agreements for Arbitration, and that all the issues to be presented were fully mediated before attorney Tim Shearin in accordance with the Agreements. We will likely receive a formal 'order' from the arbitrator soon."

"Dave, we are completing our first year at 75 Holly Hill Lane and I am now burdened by this time-consuming distraction. I've hired Marcy Bartolotti and other staff to cover for me while I am out of the office for this. It is awful."

The Arbitration

The American Arbitration Association Order for Case No. 01-14-0001-7086 was issued the following day, December 10, 2014. The Order specifies the "Claimants" and the "Respondent". The Order details a Schedule of deadlines for submissions and responses beginning on December 22 and extending through late May 2015. The Order scheduled the arbitration hearings for June 2 and 3, 2015. Other miscellaneous items were noted as follows:

- Connecticut law applies, and the American Arbitration Association Commercial Rules apply.
- The dates on the Scheduling Order will not be changed, except for good cause.
- All discovery, responses, questions, and depositions should be tailored to the arbitration issues presented.
- The arbitration hearing on June 2 and 3, 2015 shall take place at the offices of Cohen and Wolf, P.C., at 1115 Broad Street in Bridgeport CT., starting at 10:00 am each day.

Without any objections, everything in the December 10, 2014 memorandum was the Order of the Arbitrator.

So began a massive exchange of complaints and responses, interrogatories and documents, answers and special defenses, and various protective orders. Requests for additional time became frequent from both sides as the processing of archival information and other business distractions created deadline conflicts. The March 31 deadline for commencing depositions was postponed to May 5.

In the interim, the Arbitrator concluded that "the mediation referenced in both Operating Agreements was completed, and thus the condition precedent to arbitration was fully satisfied."

On May 11, 2015, the Claimants' Amended Complaint set forth eleven causes of action (Counts) brought by Claimants as investors in CEO I and CEO II in their individual capacities. The Counts were as follows:

1. Fraudulent Concealment.
2. Fraudulent/Intentional Misrepresentation.
3. Breach of Contract.
4. Defamation.
5. Oppression of Minority Member.
6. Violation of Connecticut Uniform Trade Practices Act (CUTPA).
7. Usurpation of Corporate Opportunity.
8. Breach of Good Faith and Fair Dealing.
9. Statutory Theft.
10. Conversion.
11. Solicitation to Perform Illegal Acts.

The Complaint sought monetary damages, pre-judgment interest, punitive damages, treble damages for statutory theft, reasonable attorney's fees, costs and disbursements in this action and the mediation, and such other relief as the arbitrator deems just and proper.

The Claimants soon introduced a forensic accounting firm, SaxBST, to review and analyze the CEO I and CEO II financials for depositions on their behalf. Berkow, Schechter & Co, and Chris Eck, were retained to submit facts and commentary regarding the CEO financials they had prepared. Chris Eck was also a certified forensic accountant. The 2015 tax season necessitated a delay of the forensic depositions and reports until September.

As we were addressing the Complaint and considering responses, Attorney Rubin filed a Notice of Withdrawal on May 29, in consideration of his numerous clients with court commitments that conflicted with the Order Schedule.

On June 9, Attorney Anthony Medico was introduced as new Counsel for the Respondent. Tony Medico was a client of CEO with a diversified legal background and practice, including recent arbitration representations in Connecticut. He quickly reviewed all material associated with the Complaint and Attorney Rubin's responses. Depositions were rescheduled to September through October.

It did not take him long. "Frank, this is a weak, if not bogus, legal action against you and the CEOs. I do not think there is any merit to their assertions. This could be vexatious, maybe even malicious, but we must push ahead, the arbitrator rules. It could also be a threat to induce a settlement. I would discourage any response to that idea. Let us get this dismissed as soon as possible."

Throughout this phase, the Claimants expressed little awareness of the recession and its negative economic consequences. It was often characterized as a "blip", "temporary", a "brief downturn" offering new investment opportunities.

Such frequent comments soon brought gasps and muffled laughs from witnesses or the attending court reporter managing the transcription. Coach Cohane would promptly jump up, "time out, that's out of bounds." Throughout the many exchanges during testimonies and depositions, Counsel Medico's name was mispronounced "Medeeeeco." Such episodes were privately noted as "cocaine moments".

These exchanges, and Attorney Cohane's lack of experience in the arbitration format, would prompt Arbitrator Edelstein to call a recess. The lawyers would depart with Edelstein to another conference room to review procedures and "tone it down." Many hours were consumed waiting for these recesses to end, with no conversations, just coffee in the Cohen & Wolf reception area as I pondered how partners and landlords could be in denial of the "great recession."

During one such interval one Claimant pulled me aside in the hallway with a comment: "Frank, don't get so tense, this is just a business matter........"

Before he could finish, I responded, "you're calling me a liar and a cheat! That is not business, it's personal." So ended the final interchange with a once-valued friend of many years.

On October 20, Respondent McBrearity (through Attorney Medico) filed a motion to dismiss the Amended Complaint in its entirety. The motion asserted that Claimants lacked standing to pursue their claims because Connecticut Laws require that such claims be brought only in a derivative action on behalf of the members of the LLCs that are the subject of the case.

More specifically, Respondent contended that "no evidence or allegations demonstrate that Claimants suffered any harm beyond that suffered by the LLCs. No harm occurred to permit Claimants to bring claims in individual capacities."

On November 16, 2015, a Ruling was issued dismissing the following Counts:

- Count 1 - Fraudulent Concealment.
- Count 2 - Fraudulent/Intentional Misrepresentation.
- Count 7 - Usurpation of Corporate Opportunity.
- Count 9 - Statutory Theft.
- Count 10 - Conversion.
- Count 11 - Solicitation to Perform Illegal Acts.

The November 16 ruling denied the motion to dismiss as to:

- Count 3 - Breach of Contract.
- Count 4 - Defamation.
- Count 5 - Oppression of Minority Member.
- Count 6 - Violation of CUTPA.
- Count 8 - Breach of Good Faith and Fair Dealing.

Hearings resumed in early January for three full days of detailed and assertive exchanges before Arbitrator Edelstein in the offices of Cohen and Wolf.

On April 15, 2016, The Arbitrator issued award rulings in a document entitled: **Interim Award - Case No. 01-14-0001-7086:**

As to Count 3. - "Based on all depositions and documentation, McBrearity's capital contributions, his legal obligation to make good on his guarantee to First County Bank after CEO II ceased doing business, and consequent changes in his ownership interests, do not constitute manipulation of the economic interests of the Members. Claimants have not sustained their burden of proof on this claim."

As to Count 4. - "The Members failed to sustain the burden of proof on this defamation claim. No witnessed testified that McBrearity made a defamatory statement about the Members to him or her. Based on the evidence, the Members cannot prevail on this defamation count."

As to Count 5. - "Based on the record in this arbitration, the Members have not sustained their burden of proving their claims in Count 5."

As to Count 6. - "Assuming that McBrearity had a fiduciary duty as to all the claims of the Members that survived the motion to dismiss, based on the record, as discussed in this Interim Award, McBrearity has sustained his burden of proof on the breach of fiduciary duty claims, and Claimants cannot prevail on this claim."

As to Count 8. - "The claim of breach of the covenant of good faith and fair dealing by manipulating the Members' economic interests is contingent on the viability of their claim that McBrearity manipulated their economic interests. As already determined, Claimants have not sustained their burden of proving that McBrearity manipulated their economic interests. They have also not sustained their burden of proof regarding their claim that McBrearity breached the covenant of good faith and fair dealing."

Conclusion - All Claims Dismissed

"Based on the foregoing, Arbitrator enters this Interim Award, in full settlement of all claims submitted by the Claimants, in favor of McBrearity as to all claims by the Members. This renders moot McBrearity's oral motion to dismiss the claims of the Members that had not already been dismissed.

"The Members cannot recover monetary damages, pre-judgment interest, punitive damages, treble damages for statutory theft, reasonable attorney's fees, costs and disbursements, mediation expenses, or any other and further relief in this matter, as requested in the Amended Complaint. Because all the claims fail, other damages issues, need not be dealt with.

"The CEO I Agreement and the CEO II Agreement each provide: 'The arbitrator may grant any remedy or relief, including attorneys [sic] fees'. Respondent, McBrearity, has filed a counterclaim for reasonable costs and attorneys' fees pursuant the operative Operating Agreements. Counsel for the parties must submit briefs and supporting documentation regarding McBrearity's counterclaim, including a discussion of the method of calculating legal fees and the amount to be awarded for legal fees and costs.

"So ordered, this 15th Day of April 2016, by Stewart I. Edelstein, Arbitrator."

Tony was elated as he called me into his office to report the Arbitrator's conclusions. With a handshake and a hug, he shouted, "We got it done! Everything dismissed, completely. Great for you Frank, it's the right conclusion, no doubt about it."

As we circulated through the office notifying the CEO staff of the arbitration's conclusion, it soon became apparent one more item needed to be addressed. "Frank, let's get all the expenses compiled so we have the backup to support an argument for an award in accordance with the Operating Agreements and American Arbitration Association criteria."

"Tony, I can quickly detail and document all legal fees and charges. Can I get recovery for travel expenses to Bridgeport? What about the mediation? Chris Eck was brought in to rebut their accounting expert. Can I recover those charges?"

"Frank, I believe the answers are no. The mediation is separate from the arbitration. The AAA will not award fees for that proceeding. Also, Chris was not retained as an outside expert. The AAA will regard him as a 'fact' witness for the Respondent."

"What about Marcy? I hired her, in part, to cover for me while I was out of the office and not available. Can I get some recovery of her salary?"

"No, not for this. Sorry."

All the legitimate, AAA qualified, expenses were assembled and documented in detail with supporting invoices, cancelled checks and other relevant paperwork. Everything was submitted to Stewart Edelstein and the American Arbitration Association for review and approval.

Final Award - Case No. 01-14-0001-7086
August 4, 2016

"I, the undersigned Arbitrator, having been designated in accordance with the arbitration agreement entered into by the parties, and having been duly sworn and the hearing having been had, and having fully reviewed and considered all the submissions of the parties, hereby award as follows:

"On April 15, 2016, an Interim Award was issued in this matter on all issues other than the relief Respondent Frank McBrearity requests in his counterclaim. This is the Final Award as to all the remaining issues in this matter.

"Even though no arbitration rule *mandates* a fee award, on this record, a fee award to McBrearity is proper, within the discretion of the arbitrator. Claimants were wholly unsuccessful in proving any of their vexatious allegations. See Interim Award for details.

"Based on the foregoing, the amount Claimants must pay McBrearity in connection with his counterclaim is as follows:

Attorneys' legal fees and costs	$ 211,054.26
American Arbitration Association	$ 36,880.53
Court reporter and copy charges	$ 3,500.72
TOTAL	**$251,435.51**

"This Award and the April 15, 2016 Interim Award are in full resolution of all claims and counterclaims submitted in this arbitration. All claims not expressly granted herein are hereby denied. By Stewart I. Edelstein, Arbitrator, August 4, 2016."

It was over. Yet, after almost three years confronting these vexatious/malicious assertions, it was evident that significant financial and reputational damage had occurred. The actual costs far exceeded the Arbitrator's award. Administrative staff time devoted to document retrieval, meeting preparations, and Respondent testimony were enormous. Marcy's compensation as my necessary support colleague was another huge diversion of the business' resources without any financial recovery. The travel expenses for more than two years of litigation, back-and-forth to Stamford and Bridgeport, and fees for the mediation, and the needed participation of Chris Eck, CPA, were not recovered.

More importantly, it became clear in early 2014 that the Claimants, especially Attorney Cohane, would not adhere to the detailed confidentiality requirements of the Arbitration process. An essential Member of the new entity CEO Holly Hill, LLC was contacted by telephone about the Claimants' assertions of self-dealing, fraudulent inducement, breach of contract, and defamation.

A long-term client of CEO, and a pending new investor in CEO Holly Hill, LLC, was also confronted by the Claimants reporting McBrearity's falling out with his former partners, and their insistence that he engaged in unfair trade practices, self-dealing, fraud, contract breaches and other bad behaviors.

Ultimately, the Holly Hill Landlord learned of these disputes and bogus allegations through the brokerage community as CEO elevated marketing at its new location in 2014 and 2015. The relationship with the Landlord weakened and meetings became less frequent in the aftermath of these reports from brokers. This blatant disregard of confidentiality resulted in significant damage to vital connections.

I soon reconnected with Tony. "What can we do to recover unapproved costs, the huge business interference, and the consequences of the confidentiality breaches? These costs are far more significant and could grow over time."

"Well, Edelstein did declare their assertions to be vexatious," he replied. "He had no reservations about that. But it is rare to take the Arbitrator's conclusions forward to Civil Court. The arbitration is a separate and distinct legal process. The Arbitrator's conclusions are typically the final word."

"Then we give up?"

Tony paused for a few minutes to pull away, then replied. "My thought is that we can give it a try. These were vexatious claims, without justification, and carelessly handled by the Claimants. We have immediate access to all documentation. We can strongly assert these claims: a full cost recovery, consequential business interference, breaches of confidentiality agreement, damages to personal and business reputations. All are referenced in Edelstein's analysis and conclusions."

In the interim, Attorney Cohane had quietly terminated his representation of the Claimants and moved away. In early 2017 an Action was filed with Stamford Superior Court: Docket No. CV17-6030932-S. After numerous exchanges of interrogatories, responses and documents between March and late July, Counsel Medico awaited a response from the Court.

On December 31, 2017, the Court issued its order: "The Court finds there is no genuine issue of material fact, as arbitration is not a civil action as required for claims of vexatious litigation or abuse of process." Cases were cited from 2006 and 2016. It was the order of the Court. As indicated, Connecticut Courts will not respond to appeals created from an Arbitration.

LESSON

The Arbitration...Boilerplate - Costly Distraction and Defamation

Much has been written about the problems with mandatory arbitration. In part, the commentary is an indictment of the American court system. No party to a complaint wants to litigate for years at great expense. The arbitration process is quicker, and more flexible. Both sides can choose the appropriate arbitrator, arbitration guidelines, and procedures for a quicker resolution and lower costs.

Speed is a benefit. Compared with litigation in court, an arbitration decision is reached, on average, one year sooner. However, recent studies suggest that outcomes and payouts in arbitration are, on average, significantly less generous than those decided in court. The arbitrator examines the evidence, listens to testimony, and delivers a decision which is binding. The decisions are not subject to review and cannot be appealed in court.

The existence of an arbitration clause in an agreement implies that either party to the agreement can assert a claim against the other with little or no evidence to justify such an action. Many lawyers are not familiar with the arbitration processes. The American Arbitration Association's strict confidentiality provisions are intended to assure complete privacy for all parties but are difficult to enforce.

As a result, the arbitration can be manipulated by an unscrupulous signatory initiating an unsupportable claim to harass or threaten the other party in the hope of a financial settlement. Confidentiality can be easily ignored in a manner that creates defamation, business interference, and other repercussions, without any serious consequences. A claimants' assertions and claims may be completely dismissed, and declared vexatious, or malicious, or damaging, but it can go no further. Rogue is the new vogue.

7. LESSONS - POLICE ASSAULT, 2014-2015

On Wednesday morning October 8, I waited injured and hand-cuffed to a hospital gurney. In some discomfort, I initiated a conversation with an attending police officer. "Do you need these now?" I asked. "They really hurt."

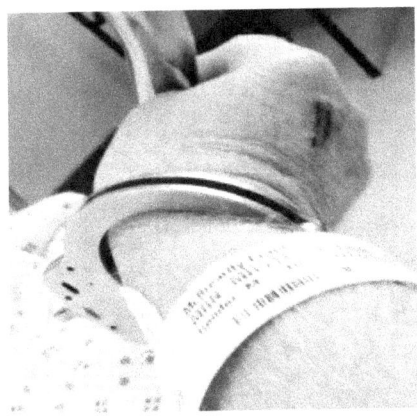

The officer replied: "Sorry, I'm not worried about your flight risk. It is the protocol. And your cell-phone will be returned soon." He paused, then added: "Police headquarters got a huge number of 911 calls from the Palmer Hill neighborhood this morning. When a 'loose cannon' goes off, it creates a big problem. I'm not one of the 'loose cannons'."

I had anticipated a productive business day as I drove south to my office at Holly Hill Lane that morning. While I was confronting the bogus claims of my former partners, we had just celebrated our first year in the new location. It was pleasant and mild outside, with bright sunshine piercing through the slowly changing trees. The Palmer Hill Road is a quiet, popular boulevard skirting the high traffic corridors of the area. Commuter traffic was moderate that morning as I began to approach the River Road intersection and the North Mianus School ahead on the left

I raised my left hand to block the sun's erratic glare as I passed under the elevated school zone traffic signals. School had been underway for more than an hour. No caution lights or other such signals were evident.

A large delivery truck appeared, parked ahead on the left, beyond the intersection. The traffic signal at River Road was green. I pulled the sun visor down and to the left as I passed under the light. Suddenly a jogger burst from behind the truck streaking across the road as I drove calmly by the school. The bright sunlight flashed off the reflective greenish-yellow jacket as I swerved the car to the right to avoid an accident. The jogger stumbled and fell, as my Honda came to a stop at the curb.

I exited the car to help the kneeling jogger. As the runner got erect and took a deep breath, he pointed at me and shouted: "get back in your car!"

"Are you okay, can I help?" I asked.

"Get back in your car!"

"What's the problem?"

At that moment I made a shocking discovery. The badge on the left front side of the reflective vest read: Police Special - Traffic Control.

Again, he repeated "get back in your car" as I stood in disbelief.

Then, an enormous dump truck emerged, maneuvering up Palmer Hill in reverse, backing towards us, the truck driver unaware of the unfolding events and potential consequences.

I pointed and yelled, "this is coming right at us. Is this a work area? Is it stopping?"

"Yes! Get back in your car!"

I paused. "Wait, where are the work-area signs? Where are the caution signals? The school's signal controls are there at the corner. All the yellow caution lights should be blinking. This is a safety issue. Look at the cars coming. What are you doing?"

The traffic officer retrieved his cell phone from his jacket and initiated a call as he yelled, "get back in the car, and give me the keys!"

I returned to the Honda and started the engine. I began to slowly maneuver the car from the curb and the officer. I saw workers departing the parked delivery vehicle and the dump truck to assist the limping officer. My rear-view mirrors captured the confusion and anger as the line of stalled commuters grew, aghast at the sudden traffic scene.

I stopped again as the traffic control officer rushed to the driver-side door to yell through the open window: "Give me the keys! give me the keys!"

He was pouring sweat and frothing at the mouth as he continued to yell. Moisture sprayed through. I was alarmed. Thoughts of viruses and flu raced through my mind. "How was this happening?......This is Greenwich, CT... really?"

"I want the keys," he screamed into my ear.

"I'm on my way to my business.... and now I am late," I replied.

"Give me the keys!!"

" Why?" I asked.

"Because I'm a cop! I'm a cop, that's why."

"Really? Look, you've stopped traffic for everyone!" I replied.

"That's your problem now, ... you ****ing asshole!"

The officer abruptly pushed his head and shoulders through the open window reaching across my waist for the keys with one hand and unlocking the door with the other. A worker arrived to help open the door. The officer quickly climbed on top of me to confiscate the keys and aggressively assert control. The keys were tossed to the helper outside, as the officer continued to wrestle and twist handcuffs onto my wrists.

After a long, sweaty, and painful ordeal under the groping cop and rigid steering wheel, I was pulled by my ankles out of the car and dropped onto the pavement. I was then rolled onto my stomach, lifted, and thrown firmly against the side of the Honda by the two men. An aggressive pat-down process ensued.

"What is this for?" I asked.

"We're checking for guns and drugs."

"Are you serious?"

"Shut up! What's in the car?"

"A backpack with my laptop," I answered.

"What else? What's in the trunk?"

"A spare tire. You've got the keys.......check it yourself!"

I was then turned around and pushed back hard against the car. The quiet walkway in front of the school had become a crowded scene. Police cars were parked on the school's driveway and four policemen were watching attentively from the sidewalk. To the left, a Greenwich Emergency Medical Services (GEMS) vehicle stood at the ready. Two medical aides exited the small ambulance as its driver waited. Onlookers lined the sidewalks.

The policemen came to the car and held me upright to walk with the handcuffs to the GEMS vehicle. A young technician approached with a notepad and blood pressure monitor.

"How old are you?" She asked.

"I'm 72."

"Do you have any health issues?"

"I have aortic stenosis, which is being watched by my cardiologist."

"You have some serious cuts and bruises. Clothes are torn, and your knee is bleeding."

"It's been painful. I want to get to my office."

After a pause she said, "Let me take your blood pressure."

The woman strapped the monitor to my left arm as I took a deep breath.

As she looked down: "I think your watch is damaged, too."

I looked. "Oh, damn. That's a gift from my parents when I finished graduate school."

A long pause ensued as the group watched and listened. The stalled traffic line continued to grow. The technician looked down at the gauge, then at me. "Oh, 185. This is high, I think we need to get you medical attention right away."

Her aides were already pulling a gurney out from the back of the GEMS unit in anticipation of her decision.

"Let's get you to Greenwich Hospital," she said.

Emergency Medical Response

The medical assistants brought the wheeled stretcher to my side. All helped to move me onto the gurney, elevate the shoulder rest for comfort and carefully secure the handcuffs to the metal frame on each side. The gurney was quickly hoisted through the small ambulance's rear doors and secured between the interior benches.

Greenwich Hospital. The hospital's emergency entrance tunnel, while landscaped, lacked the architectural appeal of its main building and pavilions. The atmosphere was busy, clean, and functional as the GEMS crew stopped at the admissions station. The medical technician rushed in ahead. The gurney was drawn out of the rear compartment as the admitting attendant advised: "No hospital rooms are currently available. Put him to the side here."

Misdemeanor Summons and Complaint

The gurney was moved to a more private room off the waiting area, and the officer departed. Soon, a younger policeman arrived with a Misdemeanor Summons and Complaint detailing three specific violations: 1) Interfering with officer, 2) Breach of peace, and 3) Disobeying signals of officer. "A court appearance is set for October 15," he said as he removed the handcuffs.

The Summons read P. D. Case Number 14-35483 in bold letters. It was left on a side table, along with my cell phone and backpack. I stared at the ceiling, my sore hands and forearms bruised and bleeding, and my bloody knee in pain. My watch hung limply at my wrist. I had not talked with my wife or business colleagues. It seemed like afternoon, and I had not eaten since an early breakfast. Now I needed a lawyer.

I suddenly felt a nudge against my shoulder, waking me from my slumber as I heard: "Are you Frank, the cell-phone is ringing?"

"Yes.... and who are you?"

"I am nurse Nedjia," she said. "Here, let me help get it for you."

I reached over as she gave me the phone. "It's my wife, Ellen," I said.

"Hi Babe, how are you?"

"The questions are: how are you? And, where are you? Your arrest is on the internet, the New Canaan Patch news source: 'New Canaan man arrested.' I am getting calls from all over; Audrey, Sue, Gina ... and others. What happened?"

"Are you sitting down? ... I got beat up by a cop on the way to the office. He ran out in front of me without any warning as I was going through Riverside. I almost hit him... then he stumbled. I tried to help, but he turned on me almost immediately."

"Where are you now?"

"I'm in Greenwich Hospital, awaiting a room assignment. Been here a while, I think. Just got the phone back."

"What's wrong? Are you injured?"

"Yes, several deep cuts and bruises mostly, that's all. But my blood pressure was high, so they will be monitoring my heart for any problems".

"Have they contacted Augenbraun?"

" They will have his name and history as my cardiologist. I'll know more when I get a room."

"Well, call me then, and I'll come down. In the meantime, I will keep answering the phone here. Take care."

Potential Health Consequences

As I waited on the gurney, my mind went back to late 2007. I had visited my doctor in New Canaan for my annual physical exam. The doctor was a general practitioner, the primary care doctor for many families in New Canaan at that time. The routine check-up had been scheduled for months to keep records current.

The exam proceeded as expected. With no changes in diet or medications, everything was normal. However, as the doctor maneuvered around my back and neck with his stethoscope, he paused, then resumed focusing on my neck and upper chest. He then stopped and looked at me with a frown.

"Frank, I am hearing something I haven't noticed before from you. It's very faint, but a surprise."

"What is it?" I asked.

"I'm not sure. It is very faint. If there was any automobile traffic outside, I could have missed it."

"What are you concerned about?"

"This fluttering sound is often indicative of a heart valve problem. But it is so faint I cannot be sure. You are very fit and healthy. It's a bit of a surprise."

"So, what should I be doing about it?" I asked.

"We should have a heart specialist examine the situation. It is possibly a symptom of aortic stenosis, for which you would need a cardiologist to fully diagnose and monitor. If this is the issue, it is not urgent based on what I heard. But it is a cardiovascular specialty, with an established diagnostic and monitoring process."

"Who do you recommend?"

"Doctor Charles Augenbraun, one of the best. His office is in Norwalk, and he heads the cardiology practice at Norwalk Hospital. I will call him and alert him to your call for an appointment. He's the guy for this." It was an early medical alert.

I got a sudden nudge from behind. Nedjia had returned. "Sorry, I drifted off. What time is it?" I asked.

"It's almost 2 o'clock, and we have a room for you on the second floor. Let us move you up there and get you comfortable for the evening."

After a few minutes up the elevator and a brief tour of the luxurious corridors of Greenwich Hospital, I was ensconced on a bed in a fully equipped recovery room. Nedjia promptly attached me to heart monitors and blood draw arrangements for an urgent assessment of my condition. An EKG was initiated. "Doctor Lodato is on her way."

Doctor Caroline Lodato arrived to advise that she was my attending physician. She quickly asked, "Please confirm for me your primary care physicians."

"Yes, Doctor Lautenbach, in New Canaan, for general needs, and Doctor Charles Augenbraun, in Norwalk, for cardiology." I answered.

"Thanks. Right now, everything is being monitored. We will contact Doctor Augenbraun for his input and advise you on the next steps very shortly. He may be able to send us a file of your cardiac history under his care. Nedjia is here with you to treat the cuts and bruises. I will be back as soon as we see some results. Take a rest. Nedjia will get you tonight's menu. I think baked lobster is the special this evening."

Nedjia began to clean the wounds and apply bandages. As she worked, she asked, " What happened, tell me?"

" As I just described over the phone, I got beat up by a cop," I replied. "What you see is what happened to me in an unmarked work zone as I was on my way to my office."

She looked at me. "This stuff happens a lot... we know it here... we see it here."

"Where are you from?" I asked.

"Kenya." She replied.

"My son lives in Nairobi. He is a Director with the African Wildlife Foundation."

"How long has he been doing that?"

"About ten years."

Doctor Lodato returned to the room with an update report: "Well, we have some early test results. Your EKG was not quite normal. You may have had a very mild heart attack. Or it is very possible the numerous cuts and bruises created acute coronary syndrome resulting in an abnormal EKG. Also, the sudden, harsh trauma may have created some abnormal cardiac responses that should decline as you rest. We are awaiting the completion of the blood tests to fully verify the situation."

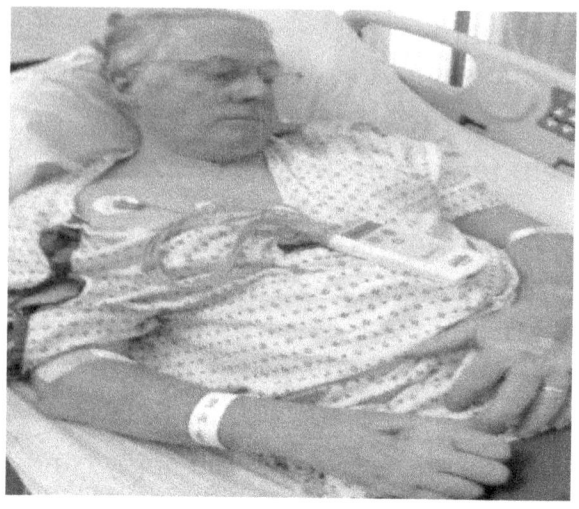

She added, " Dr. Augenbraun e-mailed us a copy of your file. He has been on the phone with us and is available for more consultation. Now, get some rest. Let the healing process begin. Get everyone informed about what happened and where you are. Nedjia will be checking on you. I'll be back with more updates."

I called home to update Ellen. "Hi, everything OK in New Canaan?"

"Everything fine. Calls are still coming in. How are you?"

"I'm resting." I replied, "We're still awaiting EKG and blood tests to be sure I didn't have a mild heart attack. Except for the cuts and bruises, I feel alright."

Ellen responded, "I'd like to come down. Is that okay?"

"Yes, great. You can bring my toothbrush and toothpaste, also a comb and brush. I'm on the second floor."

"OK! See you shortly. Take care."

I quickly called the office to let everyone know. "Donna, how is everything at Holly Hill?"

"Frank, where are you?" She asked. "People are looking for you. We have had some visitors. Marcy has handled everything fine. Phone messages are in your voicemail."

"Thanks Donna, I'm in Greenwich Hospital now. I had a bizarre run-in with a traffic officer that resulted in some injuries. I hope to be out tomorrow. I will let you know."

"Unbelievable! How does this stuff happen to you? I will report this to Marina. It is another 'Job' moment for her Jinxed records. Take care. Hope to see you tomorrow."

Some knocking at the door as I had dozed off. "Are you awake?" Ellen asked.

"Oh hi, how are you? Welcome to Greenwich Hospital - 'Police Victims Unit'!"

"Quiet! Anything new?"

"No, still waiting."

"This is a beautiful place, quite nice for families and visitors."

"Yes, it is. And I'm looking forward to baked lobster for dinner - a special treat for those in the victims' unit."

"Stop that, someone will hear you! Here is your stuff. And where's the Honda now?"

"It was towed away to a garage in Stamford. The storage ticket came with the arrest summons. We will need to get it after I get out."

Doctor Lodato stood in the doorway hesitant to interrupt the conversation. "Doctor, this is my wife, Ellen."

"Hello, good to meet you. Nice of you to be here; perfect timing. I have positive news to report. The EKG is fine, no issues. It seems some enzymes responding to the deep cuts and bruises, and the trauma itself, resulted in the early, abnormal EKG. The recent blood tests confirmed this aberration. No heart attack. We are tracking everything against your cardiologist's records to be sure nothing unusual has occurred. Right now, the heart is fine, and blood pressure readings are normal."

She continued: "I think we can anticipate a discharge tomorrow if all remains stable. Dr. Augenbraun is expecting to see you on Friday at his office. You should also get medical help to monitor the cuts and bruises on your wrists and forearms. These wounds could become infected. So, get those checked. That is all for now. Enjoy your lobster and get some rest. Pleasure to meet you, Ellen. We will continue monitoring everything. Nedjia will be checking; sleep well."

Dinner arrived and Ellen began to depart. "See you tomorrow. Thanks for coming down."

Thursday began in quiet repose. Nedjia came in early: "Nothing new to report, all is well. Let me check your cuts and bruises. They are still rather harsh and likely to be affecting joints, fingers, and muscles.

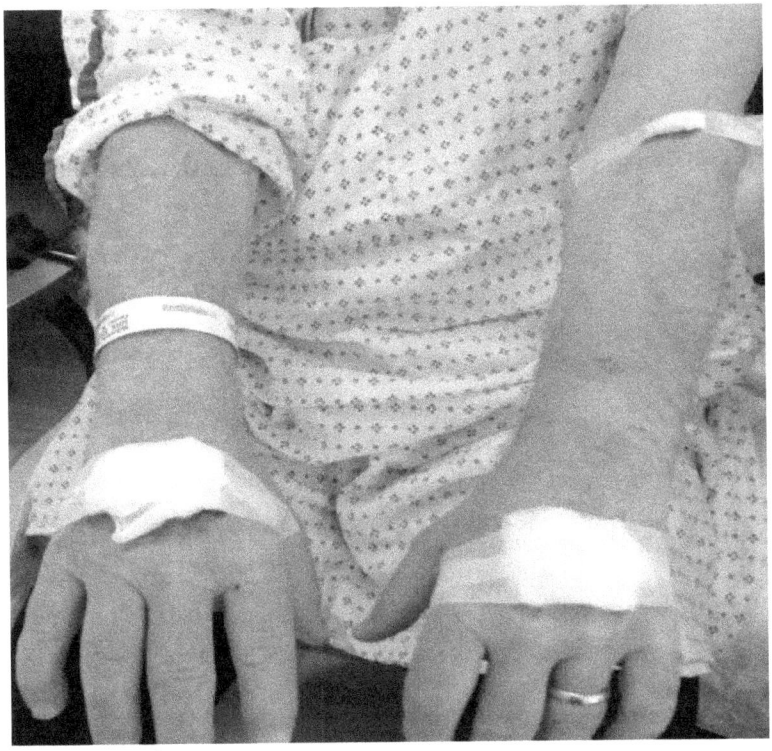

Get them checked. You may need antibiotics. I believe you will be discharged in a couple hours. Dr. Lodato and I will be back shortly."

Time to call home. "Hi Babe. All seems well. They expect to discharge me later this morning before noon. I need to get the Honda first thing. Then I would like to go by the office for a quick check with everyone, before heading home."

"OK, I'll come to the hospital around 11 o'clock. I will bring a copy of the report on Hearst's Patch news website. You'll be shocked."

" I can't wait." Next, phone the office: "Hi Donna, hope all is well. I will be discharged here later this morning. I hope to get by the office this afternoon to give everyone a report."

"Frank, we can't wait. Jillian just told us she overheard some loud talk by Greenwich policemen this morning, at Dunkin'

Donuts, about a guy getting beat up by a cop yesterday. Let me get you on the phone with her."

Jillian was an attorney in the office of Medico & Associates, a client of my business. Jill was well connected in the Greenwich community.

"Frank, how are you? You OK?" Jill asked. "Are you the guy arrested on Palmer Hill Road yesterday morning?"

"Yes, I am. Why?"

"Well, I went to Dunkin' Donuts this morning on the way to the office. As I'm in line, I could not believe the loud conversations from the cops in the back booths. They were sharing the incident on Palmer Hill Road yesterday for some who were not there. It was described as bizarre, a guy got beat-up, no reason, gross, 'a cannon on the loose'. It's become the talk of headquarters. And one of the workers was seen video recording it on a cell phone. Thinking this might be about you, I left. Got coffee here at the office."

"Unbelievable, horrible, that's what it was," I replied.

"Frank, this guy is notorious for his bad temper. He has been dropped from volunteer roles in town, youth sports in particular, because of his aggressive language and behavior. And he is not a policeman but a 'temp', pulled in for unscheduled jobs. Tony and I have had confrontations with him and his brother."

"Thanks Jill. I should be in later today. Ask Tony if he has a recommendation for a lawyer since I must be in court next week. See you soon."

"OK, see you later, take care."

I sat back and paused. I am arrested. It is on the internet. I'm the talk of Dunkin' Donuts. How does this happen? Thankfully Nedjia and Dr. Lodato arrived. "All is well. We can prepare you for a full discharge. Will your wife come down?"

"Yes," I replied. "She should be here soon."

Ellen arrived shortly thereafter. "Everything good to go?" She asked.

"Yes, I'm all set. Let's get me discharged, and we'll go pick up the car."

"Wait now, I need to show you your news bulletin. Hot off the press yesterday from the New Canaan Connecticut Patch, a Hearst Publication."

New Canaan Man Arrested After Arguing with Greenwich Police - October 8, 2014

A motorist is facing misdemeanor charges after allegedly arguing with a Greenwich Police officer who was directing traffic through a construction zone Wednesday morning.

According to a police report, the officer was directing traffic in the 300 block of Palmer Hill Road near North Mianus School when a driver becomes "verbally aggressive and confrontational" with the officer.

The 72-year-old man "exited his vehicle and continued arguing with the officer after being told to reenter his vehicle and proceed through the construction zone", according to the report.

That action, according to the report, "caused alarm to several motorists and congested traffic in both directions on Palmer Hill Road."

Apparently, the man had gotten back into his car and then refused an order to get out of his vehicle. "Following several orders to exit the vehicle, the police officer attempted to handcuff (the suspect) and remove him from the vehicle, he then became physically combative with the officer", according to the report.

Frank B. McBrearity was issued misdemeanor summonses on charges of failure to obey an officer's signal, interfering with an officer and second-degree breach of peace. He was released on a written promise to appear Oct. 15 in state Superior Court in Stamford.

I was stunned reading this: so quickly circulated on the internet; a prompt cover-up of negligence before I could do anything.

"Well, it didn't take long; pure fabrication," I said. "First of all, there was no identified 'construction zone', no signs or caution signals whatsoever. The 'officer' was not directing anything. I almost hit him as he ran out from my left. He is not an officer, but a temp, a part-timer. And it is hard to be combative when you are strapped into the front seat of a car at the steering wheel.

That is the real story. Let us get checked out."

The discharge from the hospital was routine. Written follow-up instructions were provided: 1) See my cardiologist tomorrow, 2) Place ice packs on the wrists and arms to reduce swelling, 3) Seek medical attention if swelling worsens, or numbness, tingling or pain develops in the hands, fingers, or forearms.

As we processed through, I noted the costs: "This is a $1,300 hospital experience, next we have the car storage cost, about $150. By early next week, I will retain a lawyer at $250 to $400 per hour. Talk about an expensive trip to the office. Not to mention any other costs."

We retrieved the Honda from Stamford Auto Storage for $135. Ellen and I then went our separate ways: Ellen, home to New Canaan; me, to my office. I contemplated possible staff reactions to the incident and injuries. My attire was little changed from Wednesday morning. They would see the torn garments, the cuts and bruises, the swollen forearms, and the damaged watch. And I still needed to hire a lawyer for the Stamford Superior Court appearance next week.

As I entered my business, the response was immediate: "Frank, what happened? Tell us. Oh, look at your arms." It was not surprising, given the cuts, bruises and red, swelling wrists.

Marina stared at me, and shook her head, "Frank, you are jinxed."

"I'm okay," I volunteered. "It's time to get back to work. Jillian, have you returned to Dunkin' Donuts?"

"Not yet." she replied. "But Tony has some thoughts, and he suggests you check with Dave Rubin for a lawyer for Superior Court next week."

"What are Tony's thoughts?" I asked.

"He says don't overreact to the media stuff. It will go away. We all know it's upsetting given the CEO business, the Arbitration, the Chamber, and your personal reputation," She replied.

"There's no denying that. But I'll reach out to Dave Rubin."

Other clients were alarmed. I had suddenly become notorious in the local press, with a prominent arrest message on Google alongside my business, LinkedIn, and Greenwich Chamber profiles. Is this defamation? Serious personal and business costs might be associated with this incident. Will it go away? Or should I consider other legal responses?

Without any delay, I called Dave Rubin. "Dave, I need your help. I had a bizarre and painful encounter with a traffic officer in Riverside yesterday morning. I spent yesterday and much of today in Greenwich Hospital dealing with injuries. Now, I must appear in Superior Court next Wednesday to confront misdemeanor charges. Can you represent me, or who could you recommend?"

"Frank, this sounds awful. Ah, I wish I could help.... not really my area. However, a colleague here handles these types of representations. His name is Robert Bello. I'll have him give you a call ASAP."

"Thanks Dave, it's rather urgent, I think."

Attorney Bello was a veteran litigator in Stamford. Licensed in Connecticut and a graduate of the St. John's University Law School. Dave would quickly provide him with essential background information on me.

His call came in on Friday morning. "Hi Frank, this is Bob Bello calling, how are you doing? Dave gave me a quick summary."

"I am recovering, still in some pain. I visit my cardiologist later today, and possibly other doctors on Saturday. My priority, now, is to get legal representation for a Court appearance on Wednesday. Can you take this on?"

"I certainly can," he replied. "This is what I do."

"Great, thank you. Now, how do we get started?"

"Well, keep in mind the Wednesday appearance is largely a procedural step to initiate hearings and process information. We sign in and wait. I will log in to obtain the full police report and any other evidence intended to support the police claims. I suggest we could meet Tuesday afternoon to get acquainted and share your recollections."

"Good. I will bring what I have now. I have photos of my injuries. I have the medical discharge papers. And I can describe for you what happened. I look forward to meeting with you."

"Sounds good, Frank," he replied. "Take care. Have a good weekend."

On Monday, I assembled a trove of photographs, documenting the hospital experience, to e-mail to Bello in advance of our Tuesday meeting. I called and left a message: "I am sending some recovery room photos: bruises under right armpit, cuts and bruises on left ankle, the swelling and bruising on the left arm, and my painful left knee which landed hard and was dragged on the pavement as I was pulled out of the car. Tomorrow, I will have the torn dress shirt, damaged trousers and the broken watchband that were other consequences."

On Tuesday afternoon Attorney Bello, somewhat anxiously, greeted me as I entered his office.

"Very good to see you and meet you. You are recovering OK, I hope."

"I think I am," I answered. "It's been very traumatic, and hard to explain to anyone."

"Your injuries are a bit hard to look at," he responded. "As are the clothing and watch, but at the moment, I have nothing from the court or the police, beyond the press release."

"So, what's next to do?" I asked.

"We show up at Superior Court tomorrow at 9 am to sign in, register, answer administrative questions, and then we wait. We cannot do anything until the police report is issued and we can prepare a response. In the meantime, you can be assembling information and observations about that morning, the location, what was going on, etc."

"Also, I will need your business career resume, educational background, and references both business and personal. Letters from Greenwich business colleagues, New Canaan friends, anyone from the area who can provide written testimony to your character and integrity will be essential material for our cause."

"No problem with any of that," I replied. "I've already started to pull together some aspects of the altercation. References are not an issue. I'll get you a list of names for your review."

"I'll see you in the morning at Stamford Superior Court. We'll move on from there."

The required Court appearance on October 15 was tedious but uneventful. Forms were filled out. Personal information was detailed, reviewed, and confirmed for various reasons. We soon adjourned to a third-floor conference room to wait. I reviewed Attorney Bello's representation agreement and wrote a retainer check for $5,000. He periodically departed to check on other client matters. At around 11:30, he returned to the conference room to advise we would not be called today. He then returned to the courtroom, as I left for Greenwich.

In response to counsel's suggestions, I revisited the incident scene Thursday morning to make observations and report back to Attorney Bello, as follows:

"Bob, for your information, the incident occurred on Palmer Hill Road just beyond the River Road intersection. I was driving the speed limit, 25 miles per hour, in the North Mianus school zone. A stationary delivery truck was beyond the intersection facing toward Stamford as I was driving to Greenwich. I passed the front of the truck when this runner flashed across in the bright sunlight. I was startled. I had barely one second to stop and avoid a terrifying accident.

"The traffic light at River Road was green. In addition, the long-established, elevated traffic signals at Old Orchard Road, between Hillcrest and Appletree, exist to provide cautionary traffic alerts to oncoming traffic through the school zone. Nothing appeared at those traffic signals at that time that morning."

I added: "The assailant is a 'special' with the Town acting in fill-in roles for unscheduled traffic control needs, or random overtime activities. He is not a policeman."

On Saturday the 18th, I visited my doctors at Soundview Medical Associates to determine the source of the continuing pain and stiffness in my hands and wrists. A doctor quickly diagnosed a rather serious blood bacterial infection resulting from the altercation and hand cuffing that Wednesday morning. She compared the injury to an awfully bad dog bite.

She quickly prescribed antibiotics twice a day for the next two weeks. I had had a tetanus shot two years ago for foreign travel, so that remedy was covered. The doctor stated that the unusual discoloration in the forearms, and the painful stiffness in the hands and wrists were a direct result of the bad bacteria in the blood. The pain and stiffness were now in my shoulders.

As the examination progressed, I learned that the doctor and her husband lived in Cos Cob near the Riverside neighborhood of the police encounter. She was quick to confirm the belligerent and disrespectful behavior of Greenwich police in their neighborhood. Speaking as a doctor, she compared it to a bad infectious virus spreading through police departments.

On the other medical issue, I had aortic stenosis, a slowly deteriorating heart condition, first spotted during a routine exam in 2007, and formally diagnosed in 2008. Doctor Augenbraun, my cardiologist, had monitored it closely, ever since. In my May 2014 exam, he described my status as "moderate-to-severe".

Now, after the police incident, he shifted my status to "severe". The Doctor was surprised that I did not have a heart attack considering my EKG over the October 8-9 period. He suggested rather firmly that open heart surgery and valve replacement would occur much sooner than previously anticipated. An echocardiogram was already scheduled for late April 2015.

Police Report. Bob Bello and I met on October 28 to assemble data and observations to move the Court process forward. "Bob, this episode will probably have a sharp negative impact on business, family and personal decisions over the next several months. Let me provide a little update on recent events in anticipation of the Court appearance next week.

"The police blotter report of the October 8 incident has been widely read in Greenwich, producing some rather unusual feedback. I own a long-established office services business which is often called 'Frank's business' by colleagues and associates. Corporate Executive Offices provides a high level of professional services to office clients, meeting organizers and others.

"The business thrives on word-of-mouth referrals. We can tell from current feedback that the report in the Greenwich Post has a real negative impact. One Holly Hill client called Greenwich Police after I pressed him on his rent delinquency. About a half hour later a cop entered my office claiming I had started a fight. It is out of control.

"A pending investor/partner abandoned his planned ten percent interest on October 15. He was aware of the incident and the rather visible damage to my arms. He claims he's lost interest: 'things have gotten too complicated'. His withdrawal leaves CEO short $100,000 in working capital for 2014, as we complete our first year in the new location.

"Finally, I am Corporate Secretary of the Greenwich Chamber of Commerce; a Board Member since 2007. What do you think I am hearing in those meetings, as I am taking notes?

"The events of October 8, and the aftermath, have had severe negative consequences emotionally, physically and financially, with concerns extending to family, clients, employees and others. The trauma is not going away. Plus, I'm in a forced arbitration with former partners, who were friends. I feel I am living through the Lehman Brothers' fallout all over again."

"Frank, I completely understand your situation, having witnessed other bizarre happenings," he replied. "My focus right now is to confront the police report and video and get this moving forward for you. Let me have you read the Police Report," which he handed to me with a smile.

After a few minutes of reading, I paused, folded up the report and tossed it back on his desk. "Bob, this is outrageous, a total fabrication, a pack of lies! I had an AK-47 and a rifle in the car. Really? This is right out of a 'Saturday Night Live' skit, except they are serious. It's beyond insulting, disgusting, absolutely ridiculous."

I had to pause and catch my breath. This document is now part of the Greenwich town records. What can be done?

"Bob, they had the electronic key to the car almost from the beginning. If they had real worries that a 72-year-old had bombs, guns, or drugs in the car, they could have opened every door and compartment to check. They never did. The foul language came from the cop, not from me. I followed all his instructions, got in the car, turned it off, gave him the keys and sat there hoping to leave for my office. Who wrote this report? What is accomplished with this? It is a blatant cover-up. Nothing in this, or the quick media release, has any resemblance to what actually happened."

Without any response, Bob raised a CD from the surface of his desk. "Well, take a look at this." He slipped the disk into his computer and hit play. It was a real-time video from a spot in front of my Honda, but slightly back to the left. It documented the traffic officer climbing through left front door and wrestling to handcuff the driver before pulling him out, onto the ground.

It was unexpected documentation, and hard to watch. We had no explanation as to who filmed the encounter as it occurred.

"That's what happened, Bob. That is the police 'special' beating me up. I am starting to feel that fictional reporting, covering up crude violence, is becoming the 'new normal' in police reports, even in Greenwich, CT. Can I have copies of these for my files?" I asked.

"You can have the CD, but I can't let you have the police report. The Court provides the report to me as your lawyer, but on the understanding, it is not to be released outside the Court."

"Okay, so what's next?" I replied.

"We are scheduled for a hearing on November 3 in Superior Court. I have everything I need, now, but do not forget the resume and references, which I could need soon. I am seeking a prompt dismissal."

"I will see you then, thanks." I replied.

Court Appearances

We met as scheduled on November 3rd at 9 am. We assembled and reviewed documents in the 3rd floor conference room. Bob would leave and return from time to time. Nothing happened. We departed at noon.

We met again at Superior Court on November 17, then December 2, then January 19, 2015, and then January 30. We would convene in a 3rd floor conference room or a side alcove, and chat intermittently until noon, and then depart. Nothing seemed to happen. After the January 30 visit, Bob proposed a meeting at his office at 3 pm February 5 to reassess the situation.

I responded: "I am confirming next Thursday at 3:00 pm in your office.... I appreciate your attention to this matter, Bob, but I've lost patience, particularly since much of the police 'report' went public within 24 hours, and I am not yet able to respond in any meaningful way."

In anticipation of that meeting, I had completed all the career resume updates along with roles in the Greenwich Chamber, plus college at Villanova University and graduate school at the University of Chicago, Graduate School of Business.

I had obtained reference letters from Marcia O'Kane, the Greenwich Chamber's Executive Director; my Brother Gerald, Rector of the Theological College at Catholic University; Audrey Spellman, a neighbor in New Canaan; and Reverend Peter Cullen, Pastor at Saint Michael Parish in Greenwich, and former Pastor at Saint Aloysius Church in New Canaan. My credibility should not be in question, but who knows what might be asserted in this setting.

Superior Court. Attorney Bello was very apologetic about the delays and unresponsive court process. "The Connecticut legal systems are dealing with some very problematic consequences of the recession. State tax revenues have dropped sharply, shrinking public sector finances, and forcing state and local governments to funnel resources away from the court system to other critical, but now underfunded, State needs.

"As a result, senior judges are retiring, and staff cutbacks have been instituted to reduce payroll and benefit costs throughout the system. Some courts are closed. Judges, associates and clerical personnel are now challenged with increasing litigation and judicial demands, with fewer judges and less professional support."

After a pause, he added: "In this stressful period of abrupt changes and re-assignments, I want to be sure your case gets in front of a judge I know well, and who will appreciate the total absence of prior violations, your career, family background, community activities and religious affiliation. I want a quick, favorable decision for you, no arguments or debate. The next scheduled hearing is March 6 at 9 am."

"We are approaching six months on this. How does this stuff

happen?" I said as I departed.

I got a sudden call from Bello on Friday, February 13. "Frank, I have some unexpected news. I got a notification this morning. Stamford Superior Court refuses to dismiss the three misdemeanor charges against you. This is a hard message to deliver on Friday the 13th, but I cannot delay here. Now, the alternatives are either plead guilty and accept a 2-year suspended sentence with periodic rehabilitation or plead innocent and go to court for a trial."

I could not believe it, after six months of nothing, this is what I get. "Bob. I feel like I am dealing with PTSD here, anxiety, difficulty sleeping, horrifying recollections. I am innocent Bob, that is all there is to it. What's next?"

"Well, we are already scheduled for March 6. I have all the documents I need. Your records, academic history, business history and references have all been submitted to the Court."

Marcia O'Kane, the Chamber's Executive Director, was quick to share her reaction to my quick e-mail report: "I'm utterly shocked by this ruling. Just so insulting! I wish I could help you on this. Please keep me posted. Best wishes."

Peculiar Bacterial Infection

Norwalk Hospital. The following week started slowly. Thankfully, Marcy was successfully advancing our clients' conference agendas, as I was distracted by the court response and the ongoing arbitration, with appearances pending in Bridgeport. On Wednesday I began feeling flu-like symptoms and nasal congestion while in the office. By Thursday morning, the symptoms had intensified, adding a severe headache, slight fever, and weird skin discoloration around my forehead, eyes and across my chest.

It became clear I had some peculiar infection. Ellen and I soon drove to Norwalk Hospital for an emergency visit. We were admitted to the emergency room late Thursday afternoon, MRN#594599, and assigned to Doctor Rashmi Dubey, a hospital physician in internal medicine. I was promptly relocated to an attended unit on an upper floor.

My vital signs were quickly recorded shortly after 5:00 pm. Doctor Dubey visited to check temperature, blood pressure, and the expanding skin rashes on cheeks and forehead. A nurse attendant visited periodically throughout the night. I apparently lost track of time, as I later learned I had called the office and left voicemail messages around midnight.

Friday began quietly. Ellen arrived as I was eating a small breakfast. Soon Doctor Dubey entered to resume her diagnostic examination. After a temperature and blood pressure check, she leaned over to focus on the rose-colored blotches and brown spots on my cheeks and forehead. Without any hesitation, she pushed her left thumb against the right side of my face, between the eye and the ear. The pain was sudden and very intense.

"Doctor, that really hurts. What did you do?" I yelled.

As I closed my eyes, she pushed her right thumb against the left side of my head.

"Stop it, please stop it, that really hurts," I yelled again. "My headache is getting worse, stop doing that.

Ellen jumped in. "Frank, be quiet, she's just checking your rashes."

"I'm sorry," The Doctor replied. "I'm just trying to determine your illness. You seem to have some symptoms of meningitis, but I am not sure if that is the correct diagnosis. You have an unusual combination. I will bring some other doctors in for their observations."

A second physician, Doctor Jessica Stein, arrived to assist Doctor Dubey. She promptly responded with another pair of seemingly gentle pokes to my head.

I was getting outraged. "Stop it!" I shouted again.

Two more doctors arrived to consult with Doctors Dubey and Stein. One of the new arrivals approached reaching toward my head. I put my hands up. "Stop touching me. It is very painful, torture. Why do you need to keep doing it?"

Ellen added, "What are you looking for? What's the point?"

Doctor Dubey responded: "As I said, these symptoms are puzzling. In part, they suggest meningitis, but not completely. The only way to confirm meningitis is through blood cultures drawn from around the head, ears, throat and maybe even a spinal tap. Medications could include corticosteroids. So, we need to be very deliberate. We have set up a continuing blood analysis procedure to obtain more bacterial evidence before we do anything intrusive."

As the four gathered off to the side, Ellen stared at me in anxious disbelief. She looked around then stepped out of the room to get away from the sudden tensions. She returned with another Doctor. "What's happening here?" He asked. "Can I help?"

"Maybe you can Doctor Yee," Dr. Dubey replied. "We can't seem to determine what's wrong with our patient here."

"Let me take a look," He replied, as he looked through her notes and observations. "You have a fever, headache, skin rashes that are painful to touch. Is that correct?"

"Yes, it is." I answered.

"Do you have nasal congestion or cough?"

"A little of both," I replied.

After a brief pause while he reviewed the notes he asked, "Do you have pet birds, or do you feed birds outside?"

"Yes, we have bird feeders in our backyard."

"Well, I think you have Psittacosis, a bacterial infection contracted from birds. Some birds under extreme stress, such as that created by our very cold weather, produce an airborne bacterium that can infect humans."

"Doctor, I've been feeding birds in our backyard for some 30 years, ever since we moved to New Canaan. Why would I catch this now?"

"Have you had any other recent illness, or very high stress situations?"

"Business stress has been at a high level since 2008. I've had to relocate twice, with landlord problems. Former partners have pushed me into an arbitration with totally bogus claims. I was assaulted by a rogue traffic cop last October. I spent two days in Greenwich Hospital followed by several medical visits to treat wounds, and visits with my cardiologist to monitor heart valve issues. Then, I am still in court to confront three misdemeanor charges, which are pending. It has been a real horror story, and it is continuing. My staff says I'm jinxed."

The Doctor looked closely. "Those types of physical and emotional trauma can impact your immune system and make you more vulnerable to infection than normal. I cannot say for sure, but you have been feeding birds for many years and now you seem to have Psittacosis. What's different this time?" He paused for an answer.

"Anyway, if I am right, this is easily treated. Before we do anything else, we will put you on an antibiotic medication intravenously and monitor your response. If this approach is correct, your system will show a positive response in 24 to 36 hours. So, let us see how you are on Monday and Tuesday before we make any other decisions. Doctor Dubey is here, and I will be in regularly. No more yelling, OK?"

As Doctor Dubey was monitoring the intravenous flow I asked, "Where did he come from?"

Ellen quickly responded, "He was out in the corridor when he heard you yelling."

Doctor Dubey added, "Doctor Yee is an infectious disease special-ist. He heads the Infectious Disease Department here at Norwalk Hospital."

Dr. Yee returned periodically to monitor all the indicators. By Monday, the fever was gone, and nasal congestion had subsided. The skin rashes and discoloration had diminished considerably. The antibiotic was working. Dr. Yee continued the intravenous process for another 24 hours to assure that the infection was eliminated.

On Tuesday afternoon, we had no evidence of the infection. The Doctors recommended another 24 hours through Wednesday to assure a full recovery and no medical side effects. I was dis-charged Thursday afternoon February 26, with a routine follow-up appointment with Dr. Yee in two weeks.

I returned to the office in good health, hearing Marina's "jinxed" conclusion once again, but otherwise somewhat disconnected from the business, the arbitration, and the pending Court ap-pearance on March 6.

Sadly, that Friday rendezvous with Counsel Bello was another stressful waste of time in a meeting room as I reviewed docu-ments and rehearsed potential statements for the Court. Bob dropped in: "The next hearing date is May 8."

I had to pause for a moment: "Bob, that's unbelievable, I will be celebrating part of my 44th wedding anniversary in Stamford Superior Court."

"Let's hope we have something else to celebrate while you are here, OK?"

The follow-up visit with Doctor Yee was a routine confirmation of full recovery. At first, the Doctor claimed he was not sure I was the same patient, "Are you really him? I do not recognize you as the guy I treated two weeks ago. You look different, and much more subdued. A new guy."

After a laugh Ellen added, "You came in and saved Frank from numerous scars on his forehead and prevented any risky steroidal medications. Prayers were answered. Thanks so much."

As earlier scheduled, I visited Dr. Augenbraun for my annual check-up on April 29. He had received all the medical data recorded at Greenwich Hospital, and reviewed it in conjunction with his own records on my heart valve condition. After a full physical exam, an EKG, and the annual echocardiogram, the Doctor concluded, "Frank, you are quite healthy, but your heart valve condition is now severe. If you have any episode of dizziness, shortness of breath or chest pain, call me immediately and I will get you in to St. Vincent's Hospital for a valve replacement. Don't hesitate, this is now serious."

Court Resolution

The following week, Bob gave me a heads-up as we entered the courtroom on May 8: "We got the right guy this time. He has read all the submissions. I know him well, our age, and Roman Catholic. He's just what I wanted."

In the courtroom, I was called to attention by the Judge at about 10 am. I did not see anyone from traffic control or the police department in the room. Looking at several documents on his podium desk, the Judge asked some routine questions to verify my authenticity and legal representation. Without any delay, he looked at me and said: "This must have been a horrible, horrible misunderstanding."

He continued looking back at the desk as he sorted through the various documents. Then, he declared: "The three misdemeanor charges are dismissed."

After a pause he added: "The dismissal is subject to a 30-day probation period during which the defendant may not violate any police or traffic regulations. After the 30 days, the misdemeanor charges will be removed from the records. If any such violation is reported in this 30-day period, the dismissal will be withdrawn, and the defendant will be subject to a new summons and potential penalties."

It was over. We rushed to the clerical offices on a lower floor. I signed the required forms, paid the court fees, and said goodbye. Bob waved back as I was departing: "Happy Anniversary!"

On May 12, Ellen and I departed to suburban Atlanta for a long-planned family reunion at the north Georgia resort of Big Canoe. In this uniquely inviting, natural environment of steep terrain, beautiful views, lakes, streams, nature trails and modern private residences, four dozen family members had a week to re-connect, share, and relax together.

Near the end of the reunion, Ellen and I drove to a more remote section of the resort to hike a recommended trail along a waterfall and stream. Visitor parking was located at the top of the waterfall. We promptly descended the trail as we carefully sought the special views, rock formations and vegetation of undisturbed North Georgia. As we reached the bottom and moved to the parallel trail to view the ascent to our car, we were surprised how far down we had hiked. It would be a steep climb back to the top.

About halfway up the trail, I slowed considerably. Ellen passed as I caught my breath. I had been a recreational distance runner since 1975, including many half marathons and four marathons, and hiked long trails on vacations. Now, I was out-of-breath and dizzy, and Ellen was ahead. I pressed on slowly. Soon Ellen was watching, waiting for me to catch up.

We walked together to the top. Ellen was shocked: "I've never seen you struggle like this. Can you drive? Promise me you will call Augenbraun right away."

St. Vincent Hospital. Upon returning to Connecticut, and a prompt visit with Dr. Augenbraun, an aortic valve replacement procedure was scheduled at St. Vincent Medical Center Hospital in Bridgeport, CT. The hospital is well known for its cardiology specialties. My surgeon would be Dr. Rafael Squitieri, Chief of Cardiothoracic Surgery at the hospital, who called me in for an exam on June 8th.

The surgical procedures began on June 26th and extended through the weekend, with the replacement value inserted on June 30. The recovery process commenced routinely over the next few days. I watched the city's July 4th fireworks from my third-floor room. My discharge occurred on July 6th, with a schedule of follow-up visits with Squitieri, Augenbraun and physical therapists.

Upon returning to the office full-time in late July, I discovered a small postcard had been hand delivered and left in my in-box. It was a well-illustrated request for wide community feedback distributed by the Greenwich Police Department.

LESSON

"How are we doing?"

"The Greenwich Police Department is always striving to find better ways to serve our community. We would love to hear from you about your personal experience with or perspective of our department. Please feel free to make suggestions or share any thoughts about any program you would like to see offered.

"We enhance quality of life and provide for the safety of our citizens through professional police services.

"Thank you in advance for being an involved member of the community and taking the time to help me make our department better."

Chief James Heavey

I could not believe it. I laughed as I read. Oh my God, how could I be getting such an inquiry at this moment in time? I felt an immediate need to respond. The card was rather small and did not allow for extensive comments. I put the card down on my desk and thought for a moment. I will call Chief Heavey right after Labor Day and arrange a meeting.

I called on September 7th and left a message for Chief Heavey who was out of the office. I got no call back from the Chief, so I called again on September 22nd. I left another message.

I called again on October 27th. After a brief wait, the receptionist responded that I would be getting a call from a Captain in the Police Department to set up an appointment.

The Captain soon called back. We would meet at Police Headquarters on Wednesday November 4 at 10:30 am. I pulled together all the documents, photographs, and commentaries I had assembled with Bob Bello.

I arrived a few minutes early and was directed to a conference room where the officially attired Captain was already seated with the police report, video, location map, and other items arrayed on the table, apparently to support the Police Chief's perspective.

We introduced ourselves. I asked, "Are you familiar with what happened last October on Palmer Hill Road at the North Mianus School?"

"Yes, I am," he replied. "Your misdemeanor, arguing with one of ours, Case No. 14-35483."

"The charges were quickly dismissed," I responded. "Unfortunately, the injuries were not. You have the video there, have you seen it?"

"Yes, I have", he replied. "Look, you provoked an enormous traffic episode, threatened one of our officers, resulting in scores of 911 calls before you were taken away. Traffic was backed up for miles, in both directions".

"How did I provoke anything? I almost hit the guy when he ran out in front of me in the bright sunlight. I could have killed him or left him seriously injured. He's lucky I was able to turn away and stop. Then, I was the one in the hospital for two days, fearful of a heart attack."

"You were in a 'work zone'," he answered. "You are responsible for driving carefully through a work zone. You did not, that is the issue. And your aggressive, insulting behavior raised other alarms."

"How was anyone to know it was a work zone? There was no signage, no caution signals, no policemen monitoring traffic. The school has a whole array of traffic signals controlled right at that corner. Nothing was engaged, no flashing lights, no yellow lights. How was anyone to know? It was a normal quiet morning, and school had already started."

"But you saw the truck, didn't you?" He asked.

"Yes, I saw a truck, a big delivery truck, parked at the curb, facing toward Stamford," I replied.

"That's a work truck. You should have known. That's one of our work-zone trucks."

"I should know what? Work zone truck? Really?.......Ah, look it is clear this is a waste of time. I was hoping to talk with the Police Chief."

After a pause, I added: "The police blotter report was released to the press before I could even call my wife from the hospital. It was on web news sources, and the internet, immediately. I do not own rifles, assault weapons, or deal drugs. I own a Greenwich business, and I am on the Board of the Chamber of Commerce. These defamatory assertions will now linger on the internet. Tell the Chief we had an unproductive meeting. Take care."

LESSON

Police Assault: Pain, Costly Distractions and Defamation

About three weeks later, the Greenwich Time reported "Greenwich man claims cop used excessive force." The altercation occurred on the afternoon of November 18, 2013. An Edmund Schwesinger, 76, was driving to Greenwich Hospital to visit his ailing wife when he was pulled over by a Police Officer. A physical confrontation ensued leaving Schwesinger injured, and charged with disorderly conduct, hindering prosecution, and driving while on his cell phone. All charges were later dismissed in Superior Court.

The report was starkly familiar. As of November 27, 2015, Schwesinger was suing the Greenwich Police Department, claiming the officer used excessive force when he pulled him over in 2013. A settlement with the Police Department could not be reached. The case was moved to a jury trial in 2017.

I wondered if Chief Heavey was still asking: "How Are We Doing?"

In 2017, I was Chairman of the Greenwich Chamber of Commerce as it was celebrating its 100th year in support of the Town's businesses, services, and community enterprises. On May 19, I hosted Greenwich's Annual Awards Luncheon, a well-attended gala, at the Hyatt Hotel.

Police Chief James Heavey was slated to present the Annual Town Service Awards for exceptional performance to three distinguished police officers. At the last moment, Marcia O'Kane advised that Chief Heavey would not be able to attend. "Marcia, what did he say? He should be here," I asked.

"Frank, he gave no explanation," she replied. "I was surprised. Maybe he does not want to meet you. I mean, I really don't know why he is not here for the officers."

I unexpectedly introduced another senior officer at the podium to announce the recipients and their service accomplishments. We had no explanation for Chief Heavey's failure to attend and congratulate the award winners in person before the large Greenwich audience.

As a society, I believe we are plagued by rogue behavior in many walks of life; rogue traders and investors, rogue celebrities and sports stars, rogue fraternity brothers and others who believe they can do what they want, when they want. It also seems clear that rogue police behaviors have become an increasingly public issue, triggering an unusual amount of news and media coverage.

Inattentive organizations, unresponsive supervision, poor training, and weak deterrence guidelines often enable such patterns to persist over long periods. Unfortunately, once it starts it easily goes out of control. Consequently, a certain level of violent or outlandish behavior gets institutionalized in society. As we see in the headlines from around the world, much is at risk when "rogue becomes vogue."

8. LESSONS - MOVING ON

75 Holly Hill Lane, 2013-2018

In late 2012, Corporate Executive Offices had been introduced to The Greenwich Atrium at 75 Holly Hill Lane as a dramatic, contemporary, and well-positioned new venue for the growing business. The property had been acquired out of foreclosure in early 2012, and the new owners were eager to return the building to its distinctive, corporate executive appeal.

Built in 1979, The Atrium had been the corporate headquarters of a prominent publishing empire for approximately 20 years, ending in the late 1990s when the firm moved to Norwalk. Many regarded The Atrium as one of the most dramatic office buildings in the area. Occupancy, however, remained low in the period after the publisher departed.

The new owners, Holly Hill Owner LLC, a venture of ClearRock Properties and Artemis Real Estate Partners, sought to quickly reestablish the building's unique corporate image with aggressive refinement of the distinctive exterior, rekindling the excitement of the dramatic atrium lobby, and plans to bring all essential building service functions and common area elements to a 2014 standard from the 1980s. ClearRock promoted this message through many media sources.

The building was zoned General Business Office (GBO) as it had been since 1979. The now vacant Greenwich Atrium was a unique and inviting corporate building for occupancy by diverse business enterprises when introduced to CEO. The distinctive property, soon renamed 75 Holly Hill Lane, was aggressively marketed as a corporate, executive, professional office space opportunity for legal, financial, accounting and consulting firms, all established elements of the local economy.

In the 2003-05 period, the unsuccessful prior owner had obtained Town Planning & Zoning (P&Z) approval for a blood draw "Health Center" on the lower level (level C), below the main floor, as a limited, non-conforming use under a very restrictive zoning exception: the number of doctors, support staff, and office hours were specifically limited, and subject to periodic verification by the Greenwich P&Z Enforcement Office. There would be no testing at this facility.

The Health Center space had a separate entrance and exit on Level C, limited confined parking, no medical vehicles or ambulances allowed, and no activity on the primary floors of the Atrium. The zoning memoranda of that period, April 29, 2003, and May 11, 2005, confirmed that no other areas of the building could be converted to medical use under this restrictive, non-conforming exception. In time, the few doctors in the unit became known as the Greenwich Medical Group.

In late 2012, a quiet, executive section of the 3rd floor was elaborately reconfigured and built out with kitchen elements and conference rooms to exemplify the refined corporate direction of the ownership. It clearly set forth the minimum design and installation standards of the ClearRock-Artemis ownership team for their class A office building. In early visits, ClearRock advised that the vacant second floor was reserved for a future "corporate" tenant on a long-term lease providing a full installation, and name recognition on the exterior.

Many meetings occurred over the late 2012 and early 2013 period. Questions on the C-level "Health Center" were quickly dismissed, "the building is 'Class A Corporate' no medical on the upper floors." Early inquiries by brokers representing medical clients were routinely turned away, " the Landlord has no interest!"

Soon a proposal for the 3rd floor suite was presented for CEO review. The space was too small for CEO's needs and the rent was higher than expected. We invited other options. The ClearRock executive sought to learn more about Corporate Executive Offices. He joined us to visit the business at the Greenwich Office Park address in the first quarter of 2013.

A long meeting evolved as he reviewed occupancy trends, client lists, and a long list of recent inquiries. As we walked around, he saw a fully occupied suite with numerous well-known clients, and notable outposts from Wall Street. He noted that many clients had had a long history with CEO going back to the 1990s.

The Final Deal, 2013. Soon thereafter, we received a new proposal for 24,600 sq. ft. on the first floor, right at the entrance to the Atrium Lobby. In early 2013, the space was largely occupied by the Greenwich Fire Department in a "temporary" arrangement dependent on the completion of a new Downtown headquarters some months away.

The annual rental rate for the lobby suite, at $35 per sq. ft., was a reduction from the earlier third floor quote. The build-out allowance was competitive as was the 12 months of free rent after lease commencement. A concierge service would be installed outside the CEO entrance door to reinforce the class A office environment, assist visitors, and facilitate other office services.

A large first floor "corporate" installation for the new tenant allowed the Landlord, Holly Hill Owner LLC, to relocate the Fire Department to the third floor, recast the lobby and eliminate the constant presence of fire trucks at the building's main Atrium entrance. It was a win-win solution for both parties. Lease negotiations were promptly initiated through the respective real estate attorneys.

In the negotiations, the Landlord, through ClearRock, agreed to facilitate planning, permit approval, access, and electrical connectivity for a dedicated emergency generator, screened, and landscaped just outside. The generator was a costly, but critical, amenity for financial firms and traders to assure continuity of electrical and internet service during power outages. Similarly, the Landlord agreed to allow access to the roof for the installation of the antenna system for Direct TV, another necessary technical service for clients monitoring financial news from various media sources.

In these pre-construction meetings, the ClearRock team repeatedly advised of their disinterest in medical. All "health services" traffic would be directed below, and confined to level C, a part of the concierge's responsibility. The Landlord, through ClearRock, stressed its commitment to completing the major capital improvements program to reinforce and elevate the Class A status of the building:

- Remove mold and mildew, and clean or replace the atrium skylights of the 1979-80 period.
- Upgrade the vintage restrooms on the first floor to provide modern, code-compliant functionality, plumbing upgrades, sanitary cleanliness, and expanded capacity for users in both the male and female facilities.
- Repair and upgrade garage levels A & B to eliminate flooding after storms and the collapsing ceiling panels from the weak ceiling grid.
- Elevate the low hanging sprinkler heads and other garage ceiling elements of 1979-80 to allow contemporary SUV and mini-bus vehicles to enter without danger or risk of damage.

All the above class A office plans, objectives and commitments were incorporated in the lease in many various sections. These ownership goals were also promoted in the media and through commercial brokers. 75 Holly Hill Lane would become a refined and modernized corporate tower consistent with the building's history and unique architecture.

The eleven-year lease, signed by Just Clear Holly Hill, LLC, commenced on May 28, 2013 between CEO Holly Hill, LLC (Tenant) and Holly Hill Owner, LLC. (Landlord). Just Clear Holly Hill, LLC.

was the Managing Member of Holly Hill Owner, LLC. The ClearRock principal was the Managing Member of Just Clear Holly Hill, LLC.

The lease/contract between the parties describes the space, functions and responsibilities of Tenant and Landlord in a Greenwich commercial office building. The lease references class A office, office building, general office space, office services and other related commercial office obligations in 15 separate Articles, including zoning's GBO parking ratio.

The lease/contract also contained an "Exclusivity" provision in Section 31.18 whereby "Landlord covenants that Landlord shall not lease space for any use or occupancy within the Building, or other Greenwich buildings owned by the Landlord, or its Members, for use as an executive office suite business."

The lease established a Covenant of Quiet Enjoyment specific to a class-A commercial office building. The lease also documented a contractual obligation to reinforce a high-quality office space environment for the building, including detailed "Cleaning Specifications", especially restroom sanitation, in Exhibit D.

Peter Hart, AIA, was retained to design space layout configurations and produce architectural drawings for the approval of Tenant, the Landlord and Greenwich Planning and Zoning. Loft Construction, from Stamford, was reengaged to construct a new, refined and more varied CEO installation once plans were approved, project costs agreed, and permits issued. In mid-July, the new CEO sent everyone an update:

"In the interest of continuing communications, let us bring everyone up-to-date on our activities and plans:

1. The address is 75 Holly Hill Lane, Suite 100, Greenwich, CT 06830. Building permit was issued, walls and partitions are being erected, and installation of HVAC units continues. CEO will have 60-65 offices of varying types and sizes and related support features, all with internet, VoIP, and related services.

2. The CEO installation will include four conference rooms, two kitchen centers and lockable mailboxes for up to 100 CEO Identity Clients.

3. The installation will also include an open-plan section of 18-20 workstations for collaborative work and/or convenience rentals for clients. Internet and VoIP access will be available at each workstation. We intend to identify this section as the "CEO Collaboration Club" with separate key-card access.

4. The space is first floor; easy in and easy out, with a protected entryway into the atrium lobby, and secured garage parking for all. The building will have dedicated car service to Metro-North, as needed, in the morning and evening hours.

5. The concierge/administrative assistant in the lobby is Vivian Portillo, who can assist with any on-site questions. Model office units on the 3rd floor exhibit the building's standard finishes that will be employed for CEO. Please visit.

6. Full scale Internet and VoIP technology will be employed throughout for phone, internet, TV, and Wi-Fi. We will install dual voice/internet services to insure service in emergencies or high-usage intervals. All phone numbers will be moved to the new address. No change in phone numbers.

7. We have dedicated space for a back-up emergency generator. We are refining technical elements and responding to Town P&Z requirements.

8. Construction completion is targeted for the end of August. CEO will organize and execute the relocation through Stamford Office Furniture. Monaco & Associates will be available for technical support throughout the move.

9. We will be implementing several food service arrangements including www.seamless.com. A modern vending area will be provided in the lobby.

Please be assured, the 75 Holly Hill Lane facility will be a significant upgrade of convenience, services, technology, and amenities. Thank you for your patience and cooperation."

The design, construction, permits, installation, certificate of occupancy and relocation were all implemented at an accelerated pace, to ensure completion by the end of September. The space at Greenwich Office Park had to be vacated by September 30, for a CEO Holly Hill LLC occupancy commencing on October 1.

In that period, the Landlord was providing CEO, and its marketing team, with special photographs of the building and the atrium, architectural renderings of planned refinements, and various images of the front picnic area. These were provided with the understanding that CEO would use them to promote the building in marketing efforts, on the website, and in brochures.

All promotional materials were to include an emphasis on the building. A major news release was issued soon after Labor Day:

Press Release – 75 Holly Hill Lane

ClearRock Properties is pleased to announce the signing of a long-term lease with Corporate Executive Offices for Suite 100, 75 Holly Hill Lane. This 24,600 square foot transaction is the first major, new lease at 75 Holly Hill since ClearRock took ownership and initiated major renovations last year.

Corporate Executive Offices, known as CEO, is a full-service executive office suite business serving the executive community of Greenwich and lower Fairfield County, CT since 1988. CEO provides private, fully furnished, and equipped office space, personnel support/services, conference facilities, high-speed internet connectivity, telephone, and mail services on a short and intermediate-term basis to individuals, partnerships and corporate entities wishing to avoid the capital and personnel commitments of a long-term lease.

While many in the office suites industry provide offices "only when you need it," or other transient arrangements, CEO's business model is full-service, "extended stay" office accommodations and support functions. CEO's commitment to communication, continuity and convenience has produced a 25-year record of high occupancy, and many clients with a five to fifteen-year history with the business.

CEO's office suites are used as the primary office by new businesses and smaller organizations, but the profile continues to evolve as new organizational formats, demographics and lifestyle requirements redefine office space needs.

The transformation of the services sector, the rise of the "creative economy," out-sourcing, new technologies, telecommuting, together with lifestyle and workstyle decisions are factors influencing the increased demand for flexible office accommodations.

Another pattern has emerged as mid- and late career executives set up smaller, well-capitalized boutique enterprises in financial services, consulting and private equity investing. They typically   choose an executive office suite so they can "work on my own, but not at home."

In the aftermath of the 2008-2009 financial crises, many Wall Street firms discovered a large talent pool in Fairfield County, no longer inclined to commute or pay New York State and City taxes. Many firms established satellite operations to accommodate these experienced professionals. CEO is a beneficiary of this financial recovery employment/outsourcing pattern.

This "new" Corporate Executive Offices at 75 Holly Hill will contain many of the features of its traditional format but will add large "team" trading rooms for financial groups, an open, collaborative workspace for as many as 20 individuals, four conference rooms, mobile video-conferencing venues, and cable TV service to every office. Basic system services will include VoIP, internet, and back-up installations, together with the CEO staff team.

Frank McBrearity, the owner of CEO, believes "This is a substantial upgrade in every respect: a readily identifiable building, easy in and out, covered parking for all, concierge services, car service to Metro-North, and all new HVAC, back-up generator, and security infrastructure. It is 21st century all the way. CEO and its clients can hardly wait until the end of summer move."

ClearRock's Doug Winshall is also enthusiastic. "CEO has been a fixture in the Greenwich business community for years and, with our building renovations now complete, we look forward to their arrival. CEO and 75 Holly Hill Lane are a perfect fit."

The Tour - Corporate Executive Offices

As we were awaiting receipt of the formal Certificate of Occupancy, I invited the ClearRock executive in for a tour of the space for his big new tenant at the atrium. Many clients had already brought much of their setup to their new offices. All but two clients were relocating from GOP. The little-changed client directory stood at the entry to the new reception area. I had a floor plan depicting the layout.

Then, he surprised me with a quick complement: " I'm impressed. You've gotten this done so quickly, no construction issues, clients in, a real accomplishment."

"Well, we had no choice. We had to be out of GOP at month's end," I replied. "Thankfully, Construction Consultants, formerly Loft, had done this for us before.

As I showed the floorplan, "We are responding to a new multi-dimensional market. The floor plan reflects these new dynamics. This section around the reception area is the 'boomer zone' offering traditional single-person offices.

These clients are largely holdovers from CEO at Sound View Drive. Attorney Medico here is a new client with two offices. The

Day Group and Townsend Group are clients from the 1990s."

As we walked further, "We are now in the 'Gen-X zone', a some-what younger crowd, mostly groups of traders together in larger offices.

The Seaport Group, on the left, more than doubled in size from GOP and took three large offices along the window line. We eliminated the two interior walls. Now it is one big trading room for some 12-15 traders with their multiple screens, and the TV on the wall to the left. Odeon has four or five traders in its office next door."

He looked down the hall and asked: "What's that? One big open room full of workstations and conference tables; what's it for?"

"Well, this is our new collaboration zone," I replied. "A tech-enhanced rendezvous for groups of clients and their visitors to work together. It is also the refined destination for virtual clients who will need a fully serviced office setup on short notice. It is space that can be used by anyone who needs to connect for a day. Given the evolving nature of office space utilization, this space may become very productive. It confronts the need for greater flexibility in response to market changes."

"At the moment, it's our 'Millennial zone'," I replied. "It's a co-working and collaboration space in response to the new younger crowd and the increasing need for quiet meeting venues. For many, it will be an upgrade from Starbucks and the local libraries."

"Very interesting," he replied. "And where did you get all that furniture?"

"Our friends at Loft, now Construction Consultants, were demolishing a vacant UBS floor in its Stamford building. The never-used workstations and tables were to be discarded. They called and said they could bring some over. They brought 20 workstations and two large tables all they could handle in one trip. The guys at Stamford Office Furniture think they were made in Italy and probably rather expensive. It was a bit of a windfall, perfect timing for our millennials."

"And you have internet and electrical connections in the floor for each workstation?" He asked.

"Yes, and we can put screens at the far end for large presentations and video conferencing, if necessary. It gives CEO lots of flexibility. Plus, it is an enclosed space. We can shut the doors, and the activities in the big room will not disturb other office users. Our tech room is just to the side here, for any special adjustments. Trust me, we are responding to a new array of workspace needs, flexibility, tech, services and a back-up generator for 24/7 reliability."

"I can see," he replied. "And you have a kitchen across the hall, and a private door to and from the atrium. CEO clients in here don't need to walk far for anything."

"You got it," I replied. "We expect the Chamber will have its Board of Directors' meetings here. We are also working with the Greenwich Association of Realtors to have them schedule meetings and their license renewal training sessions here. A new awareness of 75 Holly Hill Lane will be out in the market very soon."

"I'm impressed Frank," he said as we walked out to the atrium lobby. "Quite an accomplishment in barely five months, but don't forget about the atrium. We will be sure you can do big events here, OK! Carry on, good luck. We'll stay in touch."

ClearRock Properties encouraged CEO to utilize the spectacular atrium lobby for events and conferences to elevate office market awareness. ClearRock would provide code-compliant furniture for evening attendance in the lobby and install an audio system and internet connections for varied presentation formats. After a review of emergency exit provisions, safety code requirements, and insurance coverage, it was clear CEO could host as many as 75 guests for exclusive seminar events in the lobby atrium.

At the completion of the CEO space and resumption of business at the new address, CEO Holly Hill had a very substantial investment in the new venture: 1.) a long roster of clients relocated under new license agreements, and 2.) significant physical assets; the phone systems, new technology equipment, furniture, art, Direct TV antenna, and a dedicated emergency generator fully functional and cleared of all permit requirements. All in, it totaled some $2.5 million. Finally, a letter of credit, $967,000, was included with the lease as the security deposit.

CEO's marketing accelerated in late 2013 with website video tours, local news reports, and talk radio discussions on Greenwich's WGCH. The Greenwich Chamber's Board was excited to have a reliable and convenient venue for Committee meetings and larger monthly Board meetings. Theresa Hatton, Executive Director of the Board of Realtors, was eager for a spacious, well-equipped conference area for educational seminars on legal, zoning and marketing elements essential to having a real estate license.

The ClearRock executive and I had occasional brief meetings through year end. The obsolescence of the small first floor restrooms became a growing concern among the staff, clients, and visitors. Toilet malfunctions, flooding, odors, and broken towel dispensers created intermittent anxiety. Women frequently retreated to the newer restrooms on level C, adjacent to the health center offices.

Management's staff never used the atrium lobby restrooms, retreating up to the third floor or down to level C. I would report our concern every occasion we met.

"What are your plans for the restrooms? These 1980s installations are no longer functioning, or large enough, to service 30 or 40 people on the first floor every day. What's the timing for the upgrades?"

"Soon," he would reply. "I am reluctant to do anything until we know the needs of the potential new tenant for the rest of the floor."

"Is anything in the works?"

"Several discussions are on-going. But no lease yet."

"Please keep this in mind, we expect to have some big meetings here soon, especially in the Atrium. We don't want the restroom situation or malfunctions to interfere and tarnish the building's image. Not good for the 'word of mouth'."

"Understood, Frank. I'll keep the pressure on with the brokers."

As we entered 2014 in the new and enhanced CEO installation at 75 Holly Hill Lane, communications from Attorney Rubin conveyed some unexpected messages.

"Frank, please be aware these vague assertions by your former partners are prompting a mediation and, probably, an arbitration. This could become a very time-consuming process. Since they have not made any specific claims, the discovery process, depositions, and legal exchanges could take many months, probably into 2015. It's likely to be a major distraction as you are resetting the business post-recession."

"Thanks Dave. Your call is well timed. I have just been introduced to a marketing veteran of the hotel and office services world. She is departing an old-line executive suite in Westchester, and is looking for a new, more contemporary opportunity. She found our website, and it caught her attention. She could be a valuable associate, and critical support during these potential distractions."

"Great timing," Dave replied. "I just don't know how this will play out. I don't think Tim Cohane has any arbitration experience. He could drive this in many dead-end directions before anything is concluded. Good luck with the prospect."

"Thanks Dave. Keep me posted."

Marcella "Marcy" Bartolotti soon joined CEO bringing extensive experience in marketing and coordinating large conference and exhibit center endeavors at major hotels in the region. In addition, she had a lengthy tenure with an executive office suite in Westchester that broadened her experience into the shared offices world. As a result, she had a large network of contacts in the planning of events, seminars, and private executive conferences.

She was a uniquely qualified staff addition, enhanced by an engaging, energetic personality that gained prompt acceptance by the CEO staff and clientele. She did not waste any time getting started. She promptly connected with Theresa Hatton of the Realtors' Association, as it began its planning for meetings. Soon the Realtors set a schedule of 2-3 meetings per week beginning in the fourth quarter.

Pinnacle Prep was a new entrant in the Greenwich market offering expert, private tutoring to prepare students for standardized tests, and tutoring for STEM subjects in preparation for college courses. Through Marcy, Pinnacle Prep scheduled three classes per month beginning in September.

Anniversary. On May 6, 2014, CEO recognized its 25-year history in business with a luncheon in the atrium. The firm was welcoming the new restaurant Eatalian, which had recently opened on Greenwich Avenue. Chef Andréa Tiberi showcased various unique selections from his Italian specialties. All clients attended, along with the ClearRock management team. Many from the Greenwich Chamber joined, along with numerous commercial brokers from Greenwich and Stamford. A special thanks was addressed to the Loft Construction team in attendance, Peter Hart, architect for the new space, and our broker.

It was a pleasant, upbeat anniversary with many well-established relationships toasting the 25 years of business services and continuity. It also provided a relaxed opportunity for many curious prospects and others to experience the dramatic atrium lobby and the new multi-dimensional environment of CEO. The ClearRock team had installed two large marketing posters in the corridor at the vending area, easily viewed from the expansive buffet.

The mid-2014 business environment was strengthening. New clients were arriving, and few departures. Sotheby's and Douglas Elliman Real Estate took multiple offices to introduce their presence in the Greenwich residential market. Thales Trading licensed a corner office for an emeritus executive living in Greenwich.

As the mediation distractions grew, Marcy expanded her outreach to event and seminar groups. Strong interest was expressed by Alliance Francaise, Blueprint Strategic Consultants, Hero Status Films, and the Leadership Institute. We alerted management of our progress to be certain it had the chairs, tables, internet, and audio-visual provisions for large atrium audiences.

In mid-summer, we were introduced to Peter Sinkevich who was forming a venture with Google promoting entrepreneurship and collaboration enterprises. It would be called Google Startup Grind of Greenwich. He had a plan to have an early evening event every month featuring prominent regional entrepreneurs offering ideas and insights in a relaxed discussion format to rather large audiences, perhaps 40 to 60 people.

We provided regular reports on marketing efforts, new clients, and plans for atrium events to the ClearRock executive and his management team. The on-site staff was quite responsive, with new furniture for the attendees stored in vacant 2nd floor spaces, and the audio-visual elements soon in place. But, in early July, I received an unexpected call from ClearRock.

"Frank, I am preparing your first invoice for July 15. I just wanted to give you a heads-up."

I was caught off guard. "What, the free-rent period ends on September 30. The first rent payment would be due on October 1. What's going on?"

"Frank, you were in the space in July with construction well underway. We need to get some rent coming in," he replied.

"That's not what's been agreed to in the lease. The commencement date was October 1, 2013. First rent payment is due on October 1, 2014. That's the deal. And rent is due on the first of the month, not the 15th."

"Frank, the invoice is going out. We'll talk later." The call ended.

I was shocked. What am I dealing with now? I had to give our broker a call. "Hi, I just got a call from the partner at ClearRock. He's issuing Holly Hill's first rent invoice next week."

"That's a little early, isn't it?" He replied. "Your free rent period hasn't ended yet, right? What's he doing?"

"I don't know. That's why I called. Do you have any thoughts?"

"Well, he's not really a real estate professional. He's a financial-trader guy, manipulative. He's not familiar with property details and standard industry practices. He tends to make things up. We had a long discussion about allocating common area expenses. He was completely clueless about the customary formulas most appropriate for an office building with a large atrium lobby."

"What about the rest of his team, John and others?" I asked.

"I think they are relative newcomers to major properties. They may be good at the day-to-day, but I doubt they've read the lease."

"Have I fallen into another Two Sound View landlord zone here? How does this happen?"

"I don't know Frank," he answered. "ClearRock and Artemis presented a more sophisticated enterprise. ClearRock is referred to as a "Rock Star!" in the press. But that could all be marketing, without any substance."

"Oh no, it's a great building, everything is going well. I hope they know what they are doing. We have no evidence of capital improvements yet; restrooms are awful, nothing in the garages either. Anyway, I'll keep you posted. Thanks."

The first rent check was delivered to the Landlord on October 1. Their October invoice arrived on October 15. The two and a half months balance-due remained on the monthly invoices going forward. October had become a very dispiriting month after the series of upsetting events. The two former partners moved more assertively on the arbitration, a client/potential investor withdrew, and the police assault resulted in painful, costly distractions.

Unanticipated legal expenses were mounting as the entanglement with the former partners moved into the arbitration phase. The new Member in CEO Holly Hill, LLC was fully informed of the distractions, but was also contacted by Attorney Cohane and one of the former partners in their search for issues and facts to support their claims. I began thinking it was time to transition out of the business scene as it was taking an unexpected toll. I began quietly casting a net to see who might be interested and qualified. ClearRock was not yet aware of these concerns.

Mounting Distractions. In early November, staff and clients noticed unannounced visitors wandering around the atrium lobby and browsing spaces on the second and third floors. A few were recognized as commercial brokers, but others were unidentified. Several groups wandered into CEO to look around and ask about the business. However, CEO was not the reason for their visits to the property. No one from ClearRock accompanied the groups. After a couple of weeks of these intermittent distractions, I called our broker.

"We are seeing a surprising number of visitors to the building in the last few weeks. People just wandering around with lots of curiosity. Do you know what might be going on? Big office deals in the works?"

"Frank, I'm not aware of anything," he replied. "Let me make a few calls. I'll get right back to you if I learn something, whatever."

"Thanks, it's all a little peculiar. Let me know."

After a couple days, he called back. "Frank, there seems to be some suspicion that the building has been put on the market for sale. No one I know has seen an offering book or any details. If it is for sale, it must be a very private offering. I still have calls out and awaiting replies."

"Thanks," I replied. "Let me know if I can get to see any offering statements. I'd love to know what they may be saying about the building."

He reported later that he had no luck finding anyone who might have seen an offering for the property. Commercial brokers did not seem to be a major part of the process. Serious suspicions were evident, along with gossip, but no real confirmation of an offering document.

I went on-line and soon discovered ClearRock Properties was celebrated in the media for its "quick-flip" format, as in the Commercial Observer of September 10: "ClearRock flips buildings for billions." True to this "quick-flip" business model, the building was likely offered for sale in late 2014 barely two years after acquisition. In the interim, CEO had commenced new marketing initiatives, conferences, and atrium events all in support of its business and to elevate the building's market presence and class A office image for the Landlord.

As I sat rereading the Commercial Observer commentary, I spotted on a table the football that ClearRock had distributed at our opening last October. It was a spongy, white toy football, boldly embellished with 75 Holly Hill Lane on one side and ClearRock Properties on the other. The "quick-flip" game plan was on display.

Yet the building was not well leased. CEO was the only large tenant. The rest of the building was vacant except for the temporary Fire Department occupancy on the 2nd floor, ClearRock's management team on the 3rd, and a small group of doctors in the lower level. The second floor was largely vacant. Office leasing, through the Cassidy Turley brokers, had produced little. The supposed offering generated no apparent interest. Comments suggested "very over-priced."

By late 2014, none of the promised capital improvements had been initiated: nothing in the restrooms (a sanitation issue for all), or the atrium skylights, or any part of the neglected garages, which were getting worse. In the meantime, the ClearRock executive and CEO had regular update meetings. When asked at each meeting about the capital improvements, he always replied "soon."

In later meetings, after the completion of the Signature Bank offices at the lobby, he said he was still awaiting the completion of another possible tenant build-out on the first floor. Restroom conditions became increasingly important as the atrium event schedule expanded quickly in the new year. Marcy began coordinating with the building engineer to assure cleanliness.

As I was coping with the time-consuming arbitration, and the legal and health-related aftermaths of the police assault, business was good. CEO continued its growth in 2015 driven by broad marketing initiatives, the Chamber Board network, client referrals, conferences, and atrium events.

Conferences and meetings gained importance as more consulting and video conferencing specialists migrated to the technology-efficient co-working environment. Big screens in conference rooms and a large screen in the collaboration suite allowed executives and commentators from other locations to make special presentations.

One long-term client expanded his business by organizing private video sessions in various CEO meeting areas for the analysis, testimony, or deposition of experts from other metropolitan areas. Qualified local specialists for these sensitive medical, legal, or financial discussions often had serious conflicts-of-interest. As a result, these confidential, in-person video sessions with an expert could be used to resolve private disputes or malpractice issues without conflicts, schedule obstacles or additional travel related costs.

Peter Sinkevich and his Google Startup Grind endeavor was set to have at least nine events in the atrium beginning in January 2015 and extending through July 2015. Attendance would range from 40 to 70 professionals from many different sectors of the entrepreneurial economy including technology, finance, venture capital and specialty brands (such as Bigelow Tea), among others.

Technology adaptations in Wall Street's Trading sector began to impact a few of CEO's clients. Less reliance on humans and more reliance on automated, computer-driven trading platforms prompted changes at Odeon Capital and a few others. Senior traders retired and the computer-literate junior staff were pulled back to the New York City offices. Replacement clients included private-equity investors, media specialists, and public relations consultants.

Everyone became increasingly aware that no capital improvements for the building were initiated, despite many complaints and obvious need. The garages flooded with regularity over the winter and ceiling panels collapsed on the cars below. The staff at the concierge desk often joked, "he won't spend any money."

Beginning in May, the update meetings were frequently postponed or cancelled. The ClearRock executive advised he had important meetings in Stamford and could not get to Greenwich.

It soon became clear that ownership had little serious professional real estate investment management experience. While their marketing message promoted a "hands on" team, the experiences at 75 Holly Hill Lane indicated otherwise. Tenant's rent checks were frequently deposited weeks after hand delivery to Landlord's office, resulting in annoying follow-up inquiries; "where's the rent?".

The lease specifically obligates the Landlord to provide independent documentation of variable expense charges submitted with the monthly rent invoice: especially electricity charges, common area maintenance costs, and real estate taxes. No such documentation was ever submitted for these variable charges in the monthly invoices. It was not clear if anyone from ClearRock had read the lease.

Many aspects of the building and its operations changed in

subtle ways in mid-2015. In particular, the large, detailed office space marketing and brokerage panels that prominently adorned a section of the lobby suddenly disappeared. Promoting the building at the Google Startup Grind seminar gatherings in June and July became more difficult with the panels gone and no one from the ownership or leasing team in attendance.

Over the nine months of 2015, more than 300 business executives and their colleagues attended these events, yet no one from ClearRock or Cassidy Turley ever appeared to introduce themselves, and the building, to the visitors. All other marketing ceased over this period as I would get phone calls and leasing inquiries from CoStar and LoopNet, among others, assuming I was the landlord.

In late August, as I was catching up after recovering from heart surgery, Marcy tracked me down in the office with a surprising message: "Frank, I was here yesterday evening when I saw the Cassidy Turley guys walking through with two prospective clients. They were taking Arrowhead Investments and Shumway Capital upstairs. I assume they were taking them to the vacant 3rd floor units."

"Arrowhead has been in here two or three time," I replied. "We just sent a proposal. Have you heard anything back?"

"No not yet," she said. "But why would they be looking at the third floor?"

"I suspect someone is desperate for a commission."

"So, they're going after our prospects? What's going on?"

"I wish I knew, Marcy. I will get a meeting quickly. I'll see what I can find out."

I prompted a meeting on September 8 in ClearRock's conference room on the 3rd floor. He quickly introduced me to an executive from Artemis Real Estate, who was seated with him at the table.

"Nice to see you both," I offered.

"How is your business doing?" The Artemis executive asked.

"Business is good," I replied. "We are seeing some ripple effects from Wall Street adjustments, moving to computer-based platforms, exchange traded funds, etc. But we have new client groups emerging, and many meetings and conferences. How are things with the building?"

ClearRock stepped in, "Status quo. Office market is still weak."

"We have learned you've landed one of our CEO prospects as a tenant up here. How could that happen? Are we competing now?"

"They needed an office, and they liked it up here. Would you like a commission?" He asked.

"But Arrowhead will be using CEO's conference rooms, right? Not yours. We should not be competing. You need bigger, long-term tenants. If you wish to go in the smaller tenant direction, we should collaborate, not compete. We could convert most of this unique building to co-working very quickly."

After a lull, I continued, "Since 2010 this new workspace format has been one of the fastest growing segments of the office market. This building with the atrium, great parking, easy access, could set a new standard for this growing office space business model in Greenwich. Let us work together."

"No way, I've heard about WeWork. It won't work in Greenwich," was the reply.

"Hey, I visited a WeWork suite while I was attending a Global Workspace Association conference in New York late last year. It is the other end of the spectrum, as everyone agreed. CEO is not a WeWork format. It is just the opposite, refined, upscale, business space. You've seen it all, right downstairs."

"Sorry Frank. I'll get you the commission."

"Hey, something is off here. I have several major players in this new office realm eager to pursue a major investment role in CEO.

With the vibrancy of current activity, they are now asking about Landlord's objectives and credibility. With most of the lease term remaining, they want some assurance that the Landlord understands the potential of the co-working, flex-office format, and is committed to a class A office building. They see the restroom issues and the garage neglect."

After a period of silence, I lost patience, "We need to seriously talk about this disconnect very soon. Nice to meet with you both." And I departed.

Growth Trends - Business Centers, Co-Working, and Flex-Space

By late 2015, the business center, co-working and flexible office concepts were becoming an increasing force in commercial office space. The shift occurred in tandem with other business models predicated on "sharing", such as Airbnb and Uber, as the "sharing economy" disrupted traditional business sectors.

While commercial property owners were not immediately responsive to this new element, the recession's impact and other transformative factors prompted an acceptance of a new reality. While some one hundred business center/co-working spaces existed in 2009, more than 6,000 were open by 2015, and more were coming.

Business centers, co-working and flex-offices were an especially attractive option for emeritus executives, start-up entrepreneurs, consultants, and freelancers. Now, larger enterprises began recognizing the flexibility, efficiency, access to needed talent, and lower capital outlays afforded by widely distributed flexible space options.

The business center, co-working and flex models enable larger organizations to execute certain new initiatives without lengthy staff recruitment, difficult location decisions, or big capital. New opportunities can be brought together in an efficient, timely manner, with minimum financial risk.

Landlords in all major markets experienced increased demand from operators of business centers, co-working and flex-space entities. Traditional landlord - operator/tenant lease agreements were shifting to a range of contracts that customized the risk/reward provisions for both parties. Many landlords began to consider their own co-working, flex space offerings with their special brand, or in joint ventures with proven operators.

IWG Regus was the early pioneer in the business center office sector. It remained the largest international operator, with WeWork soon in second place. Regus had several installations in the Fairfield County market, including one in Greenwich. Serendipity Labs was a newer co-working, flex-space concept with a major installation in Stamford. Industrious and Premier Workspaces were other growing players.

Consultants and researchers on workspace trends began documenting how the range of new, co-working and flexible-office space providers has caused a structural shift in U.S commercial real estate. CBRE Research, for example, estimated that the flex-office supply had grown at an annual rate of approximately 25% since 2009, and expects flex to grow by more than 30% per year through the rest of the decade. Flex was expected to represent some 2% of the total domestic office market. The dominant markets were San Francisco and Manhattan, at about 4%. Business centers, co-working and flex space offerings had become a fast-growing international phenomenon.

Marketing Idea. It was October 5, 2015. At the Greenwich Grand Hyatt Hotel, the Chamber of Commerce was hosting the

"State of the Town Luncheon" recapping the year and recognizing the special contributions of educators, public officials, volunteers, and charitable organizations. Marcia O'Kane, President of the Chamber, was the well-prepared hostess introducing speakers and presenters from across the spectrum of Town leadership as guests dined on the Hyatt's special menu.

As a Chamber Board member and now its Corporate Secretary, I was supporting Marcia's role and creating a record of the event for later executive review. Many clients of Corporate Executive Offices were attending prompting waves, handshakes, and quick visits before the start.

I was sitting at the table near the podium as the luncheon ended. Marcia had said her farewells. I was reflecting on the presentations and the new technical elements we had introduced when Marcia approached with a quick nudge for my attention.

"Frank, I need to talk with you," she whispered

"Sure, what's up?" I replied.

"We can't talk here, it's confidential, not a Chamber matter. Please call me." As she departed.

"Will do. I'll call. Great work today"

"Thanks, best to you. Talk soon." As she waved to all.

I called the following morning to continue the unexpected conversation.

"Marcia, tell me what's going on."

"I think we have a unique and famous restaurant coming to Greenwich," she replied.

"Well, what is it? Why so much whispering?"

"It's the great Manhattan restaurant, Citarella. I am told it's coming very soon."

"Wow, great local news. Where will it be located? It's got to be a big deal."

"Are you sitting down? I have been alerted confidentially that it may be right across from CEO at 600 West Putnam. A deal seems to be in the works for that spot."

"Your serious? You mean CEO's traders and hedge fund teams could be lunching and dining at Citarella, a quick walk across the street? When?"

"What I have learned suggests late December or early January. But don't go searching across the street for an update. It's still very private. OK?"

"I understand. This could be a powerful new amenity for us. Please keep me advised as you hear more. Thanks very much."

"No problem." As the call ended.

I paused to digest this sudden revelation. A celebrated commercial addition to our currently low-key zone could have uniquely positive economic ramifications to all the neighbors. My business, CEO, across the street on Holly Hill Lane, plus CVS on one side, CrossFit Training on the other side, and Clay Health Club & Spa, a couple blocks away, could all benefit significantly.

As I continued to ponder this pending 2016 moment, a certain letter kept repeating. Every name started with the letter "C", including CEO's Landlord ClearRock Properties and the nearby Community Center. "We'll have seven C's within walking distance," I thought to myself.

I reached out to Marcy, my marketing director long involved in the shared workspace and co-working business. "Marcy, I need to talk with you about marketing initiatives for 2016."

"Sure Frank, what can I do?" she replied.

"I need you to reach out to CrossFit and Clay Health to see if we could establish more formal marketing relationships heading into the new year. Several clients work out at CrossFit, some others go to Clay Health. Could we create more formal relationships offering discounts or other incentives to mutually broaden exposure to respective clients, visitors and guests?"

"No problem. I've had brief chats with both on this very subject. They seemed receptive, but no follow through yet. I can revive this quickly." she added.

I was approaching the restrooms on Level C one morning, later in October, when I noticed a moving crew arriving through the garage delivering a large furniture and equipment installation. They advised that they were moving Stamford Hospital into the space and completing an exchange of furniture and accessories. I was caught off guard, and quickly sought the supervisor's attention.

"Could you explain what is happening here?" I asked.

"A part of Stamford Health will be in here now." Was the reply.

"How did that happen?" I asked.

" I'm not sure," He answered. "I think this medical group is now part of Stamford Health. That's what we picked up from comments, but we're just the movers, following Stamford Health's instructions."

The Greenwich Medical Group was accepted as a small "blood-draw" service in the lower level. Once again, I was surprised by the lack of communication, or any announcements whatsoever. Why would this be kept so quiet?

As the days and weeks passed, Marcia forwarded confidential information from the Chamber on Citarella, and various e-mail updates. The process was moving toward closure with formal media announcements, rather soon.

Citarella would add a unique gourmet food market and dining experience, vastly different from any other in Greenwich. While this 35-year enterprise was rooted in a history of seafood delicacies, its current range extended across the full culinary spectrum. The pending location would be Citarella's largest, featuring a first-ever wine store. Everything in Citarella would be a short walk away: gourmet foods for home consumption, convenient take-out, or quiet dining.

The proposed architectural style was strikingly contemporary: open plan, high-tech, and easy access. These atmospherics address gen-x and millennial mind-sets, much as CEO had transformed since the recession. Citarella would have shared market spaces, interactive culinary food services, comfortable semi-private dining spaces, all aspects of the "sharing economy" as with CEO's shared offices, co-working and collaboration.

As I was pondering these provocative ideas, I discovered Marcy standing at my office door.

"Frank I've got good feedback from CrossFit and Clay Health. They are both open to any collaborative marketing arrangements. They are awaiting a proposal or specific details."

"Thanks Marcy, good news. Now let me ask another question, something to think about. If you list the familiar, visible names in this West Putnam zone, a certain letter stands out, the letter "C" -- CEO, CVS, CrossFit, Clay Health, ClearRock and the Community Center. Do you think we could do something with that from a marketing perspective?" I asked.

"What are you suggesting?"

"What would you say to a "C-Zone" marketing initiative that would relate to the whole neighborhood? We can also include "Care" for West Med and others."

"Wow, it pulls everyone in. Has this ever been done before in Greenwich?"

"I don't know. I'll be checking with Marcia at the Chamber. She should know."

"What does the ClearRock guy say?"

"Don't know yet. We have not met much since early April. He says he's been distracted by meetings in Stamford. I will call him after I check with Marcia. Keep this quiet for now."

Marcia should know the history of the various neighborhoods in Greenwich. I called, "Marcia I need some help as a follow-up to the Citarella matter, confidentially."

"Sure, what can I do?

"I have been thinking about 2016 marketing initiatives in light of this news. As Marcy and I have looked at the roster of prominent businesses in the CEO neighborhood, all the names begin with 'C'. Could we promote this area of West Greenwich as the 'C-Zone' focusing on the 6 or 7 'C' businesses that dominate? Has this ever been done before in Greenwich?"

"Yes, it has. The Cos Cob retail district was promoted as the 'Hub', the 'Cos Cob Hub'. The Chamber, media sponsors and others were all behind it. The same could be done for your section of Town. Greenwich Time, The Sentinel, Moffly Media, Realtors, the Chamber, all would be eager to elevate the business awareness of the area. The idea has already worked."

"Thanks, great insight. Now, I need to get the Landlord on board. I'll keep you posted."

Since CEO took occupancy of 24,600 sq. ft on an eleven-year lease in late 2013, ClearRock and I had regular meetings every 4-6 weeks to discuss CEO's business and joint marketing efforts to accelerate office leasing. That schedule had been interrupted. Except for the brief exchange in early September, no real update meetings had occurred since April 2015.

It was now mid-November, and time to start finalizing marketing and public relations plans for the new year. We have a notable newcomer to add a strong, synergistic element. A phone call was initiated to get Landlord's attention and support. "Hey, how is everything, it's been a while."

"Sorry to be out of contact, lots of distractions here recently," he replied.

"Well, I want to discuss our 2016 marketing plans and new aspects for your consideration."

"Sure, what's up."

"We have learned of a major new business taking highly visible space on West Putnam that could really help ramp up visitor traffic. I can't reveal the identity, but the name begins with 'C' as do many others here. It seems we have a serious 'C-Zone' message to put out in media, the website and elsewhere on the internet. This was done once for Cos Cob, the Cos Cob 'Hub'."

"It sounds interesting," he replied.

"Well, I want to get your interest and commitment for a broad marketing initiative to promote the C-Zone in conjunction with ClearRock, CEO, CVS, CrossFit, Clay Health and the adjoining care services. We have support from all, along with Signature Bank across the atrium lobby from CEO. I have the Chamber's support plus Moffly Media and the Greenwich Sentinel."

"Sounds like a good idea," he said. "I can review any drafts. We have some big capital plans for next year. I doubt we could offer much financial support here."

"I want to have an internet 'landing page' created for C-Zone media exposure, emphasizing CEO and ClearRock: 'Seize the C-Zone' for offices, co-working, conferences, culinary choices, cross-training, banking, legal and more. I hope to get a draft out very soon." I added.

"Sounds good. Just one thing, don't mention Stamford Hospital in any of this."

"What? What are you talking about?" I asked.

"Just don't say anything about Stamford Hospital!" He replied.

"Wait, tell me more, please."

"I have to go now. Send a draft. We will talk more. Thanks." He hung up.

Where did that come from? After a few minutes, I called Stamford Hospital. "Hello, Stamford Hospital, how can I help you?"

"Hi, I'm calling from Greenwich with a curious business question, not a health issue. Could you help me?" I asked.

"I'll do what I can," the receptionist replied. "What's the question?"

"I've discovered Stamford Health has taken over the Greenwich Medical Group offices on Holly Hill Lane. What has happened to Greenwich Medical Group?"

"I think Stamford Health absorbed them two or three years ago," she replied.

"Can you tell me when?"

"Hold on, let me check," she replied, as I waited.

"Sir, I'm told it was March 2013. Does that help?"

"That answers the question. Thank you very much."

Unbelievable, the small, zoning controlled blood-draw unit had already become an entity within one of the largest hospital organizations in the State two months before the CEO lease was signed. No announcements; kept a secret for almost three years. Is it poised to compete with Greenwich Hospital across the street?

I now had to talk with Tony Medico a CEO client, my attorney on the arbitration, and an informed colleague. "Tony, have you noticed that Stamford Hospital has been moving furniture and equipment into the lower-level medical unit?"

"No, I haven't," he replied. "That's the Greenwich Medical Group, right?"

"No, not any longer."

"When did that happen?" He asked.

"I was told by the Hospital staff that the Greenwich Medical

Group was absorbed into Stamford Health in March 2013, two months before I signed the lease."

Tony just stared at me. "What are you trying to say, Frank?"

"I am suspicious something very troublesome is underway here. The ClearRock guy, told me not to say anything about Stamford Hospital to anyone in our upcoming marketing efforts for 2016."

"Frank, it doesn't sound right. Keep me posted." Tony replied.

By year end, CEO and staff had composed a "C-Zone" website landing page as part of a marketing initiative that would connect many specific elements of the immediate neighborhood.

Visit Corporate Executive Offices

In The Greenwich C-Zone

- **CVS** Pharmacy
- **Citarella** - The Ultimate Gourmet Market
- **Corporate Executive Offices** - Work from the Suite Spot
- **CrossFit Training** - Physical Fitness
- **ClearRock Properties** - Owner, 75 Holly Hill Lane
- **Care** - Greenwich Hospital medical units & West-Med

Seize the C-Zone around 600 West Putnam Avenue for health   care, banking, legal, commerce, culinary choices, cross training, co-working, collaboration, and conferences - all in one location with easy access and ample parking. Make the C-Zone a home away from home.

These ideas and others were first presented to ClearRock in the late November phone call in which he offered lukewarm support with the caveat "Do not mention Stamford Hospital in any of this effort!" The draft of the planned website "landing page" was delivered in January in advance of our next meeting.

Our scheduled February 10, 2016 meeting covered several business topics. I reported: "the CEO business is strong, but it's financially stressed by some time consuming, non-CEO distractions that I'm trying hard to bring to a close."

Management might have already reported some broker comments, but he responded: "Please keep me posted. Our office leasing is challenged by a very weak market. A couple small deals done on the third floor, but that's it. Two big buildings in the neighborhood have sold for high prices. I need to deal with that."

I emphasized, "The CEO goal in 2016 is to market the building and CEO together. I hope you have reviewed our highly anticipated C-Zone Plan which is now imaged for an internet 'landing page' and ready to go on our website, and other formats."

He looked down with no response. Finally, he said: "Do not mention Stamford Hospital in any of this effort! No mention in any form."

I didn't hesitate, "What is going on here? What's the issue?"

"Frank, just don't say anything about Stamford Hospital. Period."

The Secretive Rezoning

I went to Town Hall to learn for myself what could possibly be happening at Town Planning & Zoning. The public records revealed that the Landlord had commenced the engineering studies with Stamford-based Redniss & Mead in early 2015 for a "Change of Use & Parking Lot Modifications". Documents dated in August 2015 showed test holes, soil evaluations, drainage assessments, engineering issues, tree removals and parking lot expansions, all for a rezoning to medical. The studies had been submitted on December 16 and reviewed on January 28, 2016.

Furthermore, a major Greenwich P&Z Hearing on the 75 Holly Hill Lane re-zoning occurred on February 2, 2016, the week before we met. In that hearing John Tesei, zoning counsel to the Landlord, confirmed: "The building was originally approved for general office, but needs to be converted to medical offices. My client has tried to market the property for three or four years, but the Landlord has given up on the office market and must now turn to medical uses."

As P&Z staff were making copies of these public documents for me, I learned that more P&Z meetings were planned to confront parking details, traffic concerns, elevator access and security. I had an urgent need to talk with David Ginter, who signed the documents for Redniss & Mead, to understand the history of his firm's involvement with the ClearRock Properties and 75 Holly Hill Lane. After a brief introduction, we got right to the matter.

"How long has your firm been involved with the building and its current ownership?" I asked.

"We were retained in 2012, about the time it was purchased. They wanted to know engineering and site planning issues going forward. In this phase, we were asked to assess zoning issues and potential engineering implications related to any future medical occupancy. We also addressed general landscape and exterior upgrades to meet current standards," he replied.

"What happened next?"

"Planning issues ramped up a bit in mid-2013 after Stamford Medical absorbed Greenwich Medical."

"What triggered the plans submitted to Town P&Z?" I asked further.

"In July, last year, we were instructed to complete an initial site and rezoning plan for submission to P&Z in order to initiate a rezoning and allow for the expansion of Stamford Medical to some 30,000 sq. ft. on the second floor for a major hospital installation. The plan was delivered to P&Z in mid-December."

"Are you still involved with the building?" I asked.

"Yes, we plan to stay involved as new issues or technical adjustments arise."

"Thanks very much, big help."

The New York Times Magazine. An extensive examination of the new "Work-Life" dynamics was published in "The Work Issue" on February 28, 2016. The exposé examined the rethinking of the office for an "always-on" economy. New research examined why "team efforts" often thrive. Organizational efforts to diversify the workforce and broaden the range of staff skills were also highlighted. The widely circulated magazine added more exposure to the co-working, flex-space and collaboration formats that were evolving to transform workspace.

However, by early March, we had a full understanding of the scope of the rezoning plans for a Stamford Hospital installation in the long-vacant second floor above CEO. The space would encompass 22 examining rooms, doctors and nurse facilities, 53 medical waste drains through the ceiling, and a full range of services from OBGYN to cardiology. The installation was described as a "mini-hospital."

Jinxed. I needed to bring Tony Medico up to date. "Tony, I think I have a big problem here at the building. The Landlord has given up on the office market and is submitting a change-of-use application for medical occupancy, Stamford Hospital on the floor above. If that goes ahead, the business here is worthless. The lease with eight years remaining is worthless. A hospital environment violates every aspect of an office lease: no 'quiet enjoyment' anywhere. Clients will leave."

"And they've said nothing to you?" He asked.

"No, nothing until Stamford Medical was seen moving downstairs. All he said was 'don't mention Stamford Hospital to anyone'. Also, no capital improvements since we moved in. Now I know why. And I suspect many commercial brokers have been aware of this for months, possibly since the building was up for sale."

"You better get me a copy of the lease. Who did it, and who reviewed it for CEO?" He asked.

"The lease was prepared by Robinson & Cole for the Landlord, and Steve Steinmetz reviewed it for the LLC. I'll get a copy made for you right away."

"Great, I'll go over it with Steve and get his feedback. Something must have been discussed about these issues," he replied.

After a pause, "damn, how does this stuff happen? SoundView, GOP, arbitration, cop assault, now this. The arbitration is almost over. But I can't explain this stuff to anyone."

"Well, the ladies think you're jinxed. Marina says you're Job, from the bible."

It was now clear why nothing had been done to upgrade fundamental aspects of the building in accordance with contractual obligations, or in response to tenant complaints. And there had been no ClearRock participation in marketing or atrium events after 2014.

Management Neglect - Contract Breaches. The photographic evidence of the three years documented the story. Basic provisions of the lease were ignored.

T

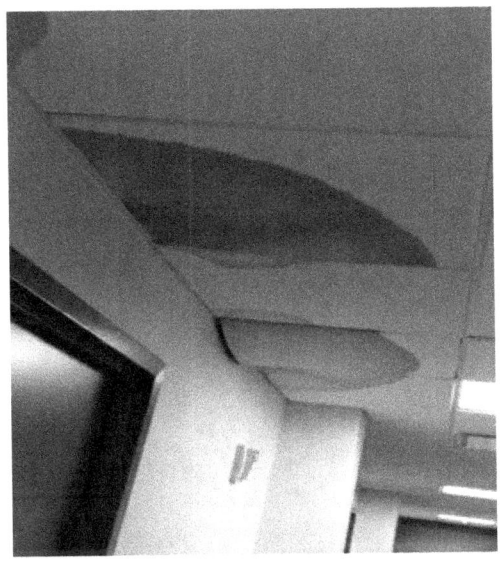

The long-promised upgrades to the "class A" office building never happened. The dramatic atrium skylights remained covered with mold and mildew.

In early March several phone calls, messages, and e-mail memoranda were directed to ClearRock with the desire for a meeting to address the fact that the Tenant/CEO had signed a detailed commercial office lease for space in a GBO building. The restrictive variances of 2003-05 did not apply to any location in the three main office floors, as set forth in the Town P&Z Department's public records. We had relied on that, and their repeated assertions "no interest in medical."

"The plans for the hospital installation severely conflict with the lease, the CEO business model, and any sense of a class A office environment. The value of CEO's 28-year shared office suite business and the lease with eight years left will vanish. We have a meeting scheduled for March 15. Let's talk this through."

He quickly responded: "Frank, what you've written and said is 'revisionist history', pay your rent and we will work this out. See you then."

"Hey, we've been marketing the GBO building, with your encouragement, for our mutual benefit, especially the atrium conferences. The CEO business benefited, but nobody from ClearRock or Cassidy Turley ever appeared. And no upgrades; we have cleaned the restrooms for the atrium events. Why were we kept in the dark? I need answers here for partners and clients."

"That's 'revisionist history' Frank. That's all I can say. We'll talk soon."

Follow-up calls were unproductive. The ClearRock executive did call to advise he could not make the March 15 meeting, as he was busy in Stamford. With that communication, Attorney Medico and I agreed that a more assertive stance was needed. Monthly rental payments were suspended until we had some more detailed communications with the Landlord.

Attorney Medico reported our decision to Landlord's attorney with Robinson & Cole, and that a $250,000 trust account had been established, under Medico's control, to assure full rent recovery if timely discussions take place.

Holly Hill Owner, LLC suddenly took very assertive actions against CEO Holly Hill, LLC in early April, with no prior notice. The Landlord drew down the entire letter-of-credit, $967,000, even though the delinquency was a small fraction of that total and covered by the Medico trust account. The draw-down occurred in two installments on April 5 and 7 as the Bank initially objected to the total because the withdrawal requests were substantially more than the delinquency amount and conflicted with other provisions of Tenant's lease with respect to the security deposit.

The banker who succumbed to the pressure from Landlord's litigation counsel quietly left Patriot Bank soon thereafter. It seemed obvious that the Landlord needed the entire $967,000 to fund the pending site work, drainage, excavation, and parking expansions required under the P&Z plan quietly engineered by Redniss & Mead over the prior years.

History was repeating. I grabbed Tony. "I can't believe it. Greenwich Office Park did the same thing. We found it took down the entire CEO letter of credit to pay leasing commissions to its brokers. What is going on?" No answer.

At the same time, we were trying to obtain some understanding as to how CEO could function in a medical building, and what were the Landlord's plans for both a hospital and class A offices in the same building? A May 3 meeting was scheduled to address this question. Lawyers for both parties accompanied their clients in the CEO conference room to hear the explanation from ClearRock.

His response was very quick. "We are planning for a unique and dramatic reconfiguration of the building, creating a separate GBO office element visually and physically distinct from the medical, with separate entrances and exits, lobby services, elevator access, parking garages, and security features. Signage will reflect a uniquely 'bifurcated' building at 75 Holly Hill Lane. Architectural plans are in development. We expect it will offer a unique two-dimensional platform."

When asked a few days later to confirm these plans in writing, ClearRock did not respond. We had alerted architectural and engineering advisors for some assistance in the review. We pressed again for any possible architectural and/or engineering documents to illustrate the concepts for our review. ClearRock remained unresponsive.

Finally, when Attorney Medico later queried Landlord's counsel on this matter by phone, he was told: "No such plans existed. It was off the top of his head. Nothing of the sort actually existed or was even being considered."

The attorney then added: "By the way, Tony, there is nothing in the lease to prevent this shift to medical on the second floor. The 'Merger Clause' in the lease affirms the Connecticut Statute that all such understandings must be written in the document. The lease does not cite any prohibitions regarding medical or non-GBO uses, regardless of what was promoted in the media or said in meetings."

Tony was stunned, and soon pulled me into his office: "Frank, Landlord's counsel has reported no 'bifurcation' plans exist, never did. It's all bullshit!"

I could hardly control the anger. "Tony, I was told early-on that he just makes things up, total fakery. Uh-oh, he's a liar. I have been working through a shift from 'Big Short' to 'Quick Flip' to 'Revisionist History', or 'Fake News'. That is what's going on here, right? And my business is now worthless."

Tony then asked: "Are you aware of the 'Merger Clause' in your lease here?"

"No. What's that?"

"It's a 'boilerplate' three sentence clause buried on page 38 that says the lease is the entire agreement between the parties. It dismisses all statements, assertions or promises made outside the lease, but not included in it. What is written in the lease is the deal," he said.

"The lease is a contract involving class A office space. All the details are for office tenants, building management and operations, upgrades, environment, 'quiet enjoyment', cleanliness, activities, etc.," I replied.

"It doesn't say Landlord can't go medical."

"So? Medical is in direct conflict with an office lease, just like a hotel, or assisted living. I do not understand. There are 15 specific provisions reinforcing a commitment to a high-quality building for commercial office tenants."

"Did you go over this with Steve?" He asked.

"No," I replied. "This kind of discussion never happened."

"Let me talk with Steve. Landlord's counsel believes the Merger Clause is their escape hatch out of the lease with CEO."

I retrieved the lease from my files of Holly Hill documents. The Agreement of Lease, signed on May 28, 2013, was a 43-page document with an additional 30 pages of Exhibits and Schedules detailing office cleaning specifications, building rules and regulations, and other specifics of office space occupancy and services.

Page 38 contained "Section 31.7. Merger; Written Supplements. This Lease contains the entire agreement between the parties and supersedes all prior understandings, if any, with respect thereto. The lease shall not be modified, changed, or supplemented except by a written instrument executed by both parties. All references in this Lease to the consent or approval of Landlord shall be deemed to mean the written consent or approval of Landlord and no consent or approval of Landlord shall be effective for any purpose unless such consent or approval is set forth in a written instrument executed by Landlord."

It was one small paragraph in a commercial office lease of more than 70 pages. What was going on? At that moment, any conscientious professional relationship with the Landlord ended. It had become abundantly clear that CEO was brought to the grand first floor opportunity to pay rent, elevate awareness and augment the marketing to the office sector. The 2014 "quick flip" had done something.

Attorney Medico soon confirmed the extent of discussions about the Merger Clause in the lease. "Frank, I talked with Steve. He said it didn't come up."

"That's my recollection. So, are you suggesting it is an important provision that was overlooked? Again, fifteen specific class A office provisions. Right?"

"Yes. But I don't know. They may be vulnerable here," he replied.

"Well, what's the statute-of-limitations for something like this?"

"Three years." He answered.

"We're too late. The lease was signed in late May 2013. It is now June 2016. Let's drop that for the time being."

"And Tony, I'm not getting any response from the three investor prospects who were interested in the business. They know. Word has been out. I'm at a loss."

The Holly Hill owners had no long-term office building owner-ship or management plan. It was viewed an easy, post-recession, low-budget acquisition to quickly lease and sell. When the goal of a brief, profitable office investment failed in 2014, all office lease requirements, and professional obligations ended.

A Town Planning and Zoning meeting on May 3 approved the final site plan resolution subject to several requirements de-tailed in a May 17 letter. Exterior excavation and demolition efforts commenced quickly to expand the exterior surface parking to comply with medical zoning requirements. All clients and visitors became informed and visibly aware of the dramatic, intrusive changes underway. The inviting picnic area was removed to expand the parking out front.

The mini-hospital installation soon commenced on the floor above with the immediate need to insert the 53 medical waste drains through the ceiling areas above the CEO space. The noise level was often intense, and weekend efforts deposited debris everywhere. After considerable construction, noise and interference with client activities, Stamford Hospital began to take occupancy of the 33,000 square feet on the second floor.

Some clients departed and others simply stopped paying their monthly rent obligation. New client inquiries declined. The occasional new client signed in at a much lower rent than its predecessor, and for a much shorter term. Most existing clients took a wait and see attitude while looking elsewhere. Monthly revenue declined, and long-standing client relationships fell into anger and disbelief.

Court Confrontation - Eviction

Holly Hill Owner, LLC then took an aggressive stance to evict Tenant from the building for rent defaults, and failure to replace the letter-of-credit. It initiated a legal claim against CEO Holly Hill, LLC, in Norwalk Superior Court, to retrieve the 24,600 sq. ft. from the lease, and quickly take possession of Tenant's other assets: the mounting receivables, technology, and equipment installations that could remain to serve the entire building.

CEO and Medico & Associates promptly arranged for a large roster of well-informed witnesses, including the architect, contractor, broker, clients, and experts on the requisite shared-workspace environment. Ray Lindenberg, Founder and President of the Workspace Association of New York, and a 25-year veteran of the business center workspace industry, offered the most specific and experienced commentary for the Court's consideration:

- "Individuals and companies rent space at business centers to outsource their business space needs. The most important requirement of that decision is the corresponding commitment that a professional, secure, and inviting business environment will be provided and sustained.
- An event that interferes with that commitment disrupts the core element of the agreements, and damages the businesses, client relationships, and income at all levels. In the case of an unexpected conversion to medical usage, clients and visitors will not wish to intermingle with an infirmed population, with the potential for contagious pathogens and medical waste circulating in the building's environment.
- The resulting departure from the professional business atmosphere in the atrium lobby, and the presence of ambulances and ambulatory patients in the entryways and parking lots, will eliminate the building's appeal to professional businesses, their clients and personnel."

Medico & Associates assembled an extensive legal presentation for the Court, including scores of exhibits, in addition to the lease contract, that confirmed Landlord's expressed commitment to office space, in order to confront Landlord's assertions as egregious distortions of facts and circumstances. The resulting financial consequences to the Tenant were to be submitted in detail.

Segments of the presentations were provided in advance for review before finalization and delivery to the Court. After several hours of reading through drafts, I needed to talk with Counsel. "Tony, much of this is familiar to me. It is right out of Attorney Rubin's submission opposing Clarion, CBRE and the GOP Landlord: confidentiality breaches, contract defaults, bad faith, and this Unfair Trade Practices Act. This is a repeat of 2012. Chamber members and other associates in the area have been alerting me to "CUTPA" frequently over this period. Why am I fighting this stuff?"

"Frank, I wish I had an answer for you, without repeating staff's frequent 'jinxed' response. This is the situation, and the legal response procedure is established in civil court. We need to press through it. But now we must circumvent the Merger Clause. Then we can get to the bigger context."

Counsel responded with a Complaint and an Action in Norwalk Superior Court against Holly Hill Owner LLC, and JustClear Holly Hill, LLC, Docket No. NWH- CV-17-6002424-S. Counsel asserted a strong and compelling case for the Defendant's Application for Pre-Judgment Remedy:

- Breach of Contract based upon Promissory Estoppel and Detrimental Reliance,
- Violation of Connecticut Unfair Trade Practices Act ("CUTPA"),
- Breach of Contract based on Covenant of Quiet Enjoyment,
- Breach of Contract based on Unjust Enrichment,
- Breach of Covenant of Good Faith and Fair Dealing (Fraud), and
- Pre-Judgment Remedy (PJR) to recover losses and legal

fees ($2,775,000).

The Complaint was authorized on August 1, 2016, and promptly delivered to Judge Edward Rodriguez in Norwalk Superior Court, Housing Session, along with scores of supporting documents. The first Summary Process Hearings were scheduled for August 16 and 18.

The August appearances introduced the participants to the Court and Judge Rodriguez. Landlord's counsel for the Plaintiff was a partner with DePanfilis & Vallerie, a prominent and active law firm in Norwalk Superior Court. Tenant's counsel quickly endeavored to inform the Court, and Judge Rodriguez, of the fundamental elements of the business of Corporate Executive Offices and its reliance on a secure, clean, professional office environment for its clientele.

Landlord's counsel forcefully objected to these witness testimonies as irrelevant and unnecessary. "The rezoning only involves the second floor," he would shout. "It has no impact on the first floor. Plaintiff plans to block out the atrium so that Tenant's clients and visitors will not see or hear the activities above." Brief memories of the earlier "bifurcation" assertions surfaced frequently.

He often added with emphasis, "Furthermore, there is nothing in the lease about medical. It is not prohibited in the lease. If there was a prohibition, it should have been written into the lease per Connecticut Code." Judge Rodriguez accepted these objections without any discussion. The quick responses reminded us of random lawyer comments in the Court's waiting area about "a 40-second attention span."

It became clear to Attorney Medico, and others, that Judge Rodriguez had an incomplete understanding of the Tenant's business model, the specific office lease obligations in support of the business, and what was presented to Tenant in the lease negotiations. The many written expressions of mutual interest and financial commitment to a class A office environment were detailed in the lease and elsewhere. All were provided in the documents presented to the Court in early August.

As a result, Medico sought a meeting with Judge Rodriguez and his staff to confirm all documents were received and answer any questions. A meeting was scheduled for all parties on October 4, 2016 at 10 am. Tony and I arrived early for the briefing, with a large box of additional records in support of the discussion. We announced our arrival for Judge Rodriguez with the receptionist and waited.

In early afternoon, the Landlord's attorney approached us in the reception area to advise that the Judge had not yet reviewed the documents. The meeting had to be postponed. However, it never occurred, not even for a "40-second" exchange.

Hearings resumed on December 8 in which the ClearRock executive testified on behalf of the Plaintiffs. He asserted that "medical occupied more than 20,000 sq. ft., or more than 20 percent of the building, when it was acquired out of foreclosure in 2012. Medical was the single prime tenant."

CEO's Counsel offered a correction, "the real facts are 11,040 sq. ft., and less than 10 percent of the building. Moreover, the activities were very restricted and subject to Greenwich Planning and Zoning review and approval."

He replied, "That's not the situation in 2012 when we bought it. Medical was more than 20,000 sq. ft."

Defendant's counsel responded, "Town records show 11,040 sq. ft., nothing more. Is the Greenwich Fire Department's temporary occupancy in your total?"

Recollections of "revisionist history" and "fake news" surfaced again, as the ClearRock executive did not respond further.

The executive's subsequent private deposition on February 1, 2017, in the offices of Landlord's legal counsel in Norwalk, added little substance to earlier testimony, or his role with the investment. In his deposition, he acknowledged that he had read little of the lease agreement with CEO Holly Hill, LLC. When asked to read various articles in the lease, he discovered he had forgotten his eyeglasses. The attending court stenographer loaned his glasses to help.

He acknowledged he did not prepare or review the rent invoice statements sent to CEO Holly Hill, LLC, and was not sure who performed this administrative work. He could not name the bank to which rent checks were deposited, or the specific bank account.

Hearings resumed on May 23 and again on July 11. The Landlord promptly secured a Summary Process eviction notice from Norwalk Superior Court, Housing Session, with the following explanation: "Defendant failed to meet its burden of proof on any of its Special Defenses. The evidence relates to its claimed reliance on verbal statements by Plaintiff that it would not rent the second floor to a medical provider. Those pre-lease statements are not in the lease and should have been to be enforceable per Connecticut General Statute Sec. 52-550."

Statute Sec. 52-550 references the Merger Clause in a contract. Judge Rodriguez's statement made no mention of the office lease contract, Connecticut Statute Sec. 42-110b (CUTPA) or the PJR for financial recovery. As a result of the brief ruling, CEO Holly Hill, LLC would be evicted from its premises.

On July 18, 2017, a bold headline and photograph appeared in the Greenwich Time newspaper - **"Greenwich Office Building Fetches $34M Price Tag"**

"A Greenwich office building sold for $33.8 million last week according to documents filed at Greenwich Town Hall, with plans in place to convert some of the space for medical use. The three-story structure at 75 Holly Hill Lane includes more than 100,000 square feet and was built in 1979. Following the recession, the building underwent foreclosure and New York

City - based ClearRock Properties working with Artemis Real Estate bought it from the lender for $19.3 million in 2012. Last week, New York City - based Benedict Realty Group inked a nearly $34 million deal for the office building. Neither ClearRock nor BRG responded to requests for comment

"At the time ClearRock Properties took over the building, it was about 20 percent leased, according to its website. ClearRock managing principal Doug Winshall told Hearst Connecticut Media in 2012 he foresaw the offices eventually housing financial services companies, law firms and accountants.

"Over the last few years, plans have arisen to convert some of the office building for medical use with Stamford Health Medical Group expanding onto its second floor. Stamford Health has had a limited presence at 75 Holly Hill Lane since 2013, according to hospital spokesman Craig Andrews, when a private practice operating there joined its physical network.

"Last year, Greenwich's Planning and Zoning Commission approved plans to renovate portions of the building and parking areas to accommodate dramatic growth in Stamford Health's footprint there. Construction is underway to turn the second floor into more medical offices and exam rooms.

"In total, roughly 33,000 square feet of the building will eventually be occupied by the medical group, which will offer primary care physicians along with specialists in cardiology, endocrinology, neurology, gastroenterology, orthopedics, rheumatology, gynecology and neurosurgery, Andrews said. Patients will also be able to visit the location for personalized health and preventive care services, X-ray, ultrasound, bone density testing, screening mammography and cardiology testing. The medical expansion is expected to be completed by this fall, according to Andrews.

"Stamford Health adds to the increasing variety of medical options positioned nearby, which include Greenwich Hospital and WestMed Medical Group. The building's pivot to increased medical uses came after ClearRock marketed it to office tenants for several years without as much success, according to discussions during planning and zoning meetings last year.

"Mixing a building between offices and medical uses can be a 'tricky situation' said Christian Bangert of Rhys, a Stamford - based commercial real estate company. 'There are things that come with medical that don't always mesh with offices, such as heavier traffic flow, additional wear and tear on the building and potentially sick visitors sharing space with office tenants,' he said. 'I know some tenants in the building who will probably not be happy with Stamford Hospital moving in,' Bangert said.

"But the medical tenant is likely what helped attract last week's buyer, Bangert added, as another of BRG's recent acquisitions includes a 60 million portfolio of medical office buildings in Rhode Island. 'BRG will continue to expand its medical office portfolio along the East Coast in the upcoming years,' BRG principal Daniel Benedict said in a statement about the deal."

Attempts to reconvene the case in the Judge's hearing room were unsuccessful. Judge Rodriguez's retirement from Norwalk Superior Court was quietly announced soon thereafter. The 28-year business of Corporate Executive Offices would be closing on October 31, 2017. I would also be resigning as Chairman of the Greenwich Chamber of Commerce as the business closed.

We began to quickly implement the removal of physical assets from the office suite. Numerous prints from the early purchase, along with newer artworks added for Holly Hill, were rushed to storage. The conference room chairs and tables were donated to the Greenwich YWCA and other furniture items, to local non-profit groups. Efforts to sell and relocate the separately installed CEO generator, engaged for just one brief interval in 2016, were unproductive. The relocation costs were prohibitive. It would remain to serve the building.

Soon after, I met with Steve Steinmetz to advise him, in person, about Judge Rodriguez's July decision and all the background circumstances. He was visibly shaken and said: "I can't believe this. You got no notice. You have gotten no consideration for the lease. Nothing! I have never encountered this set of circumstances in my career. Nothing like this anywhere in this market. This is really bad behavior."

"Steve, I've been in the real estate investment world for more than 25 years, and I haven't ever witnessed it either. Stamford Hospital was in there for 2 to 3 months before the lease was signed. We knew nothing for almost 3 years," I replied as he sat there and stared at the Judge's one-page decision in disbelief. It was a sad moment, as Steve had been the contract attorney for CEO since 2007.

The completely unexpected turn of events was devastating. The "shared-offices/co-working" industry was evolving in the manner of Airbnb, Uber, Lyft, and others in this new "sharing economy" entrepreneurial world. These planned office environments providing professional, supported workspace "where, when and how" clients (or members) need it, had grown to more than 10,000 facilities worldwide, a three-fold increase since 2013. Yet, the Landlord was unresponsive.

In retrospect, Redniss & Mead, the Stamford based engineering firm, was engaged in 2013 to study site engineering, zoning aspects, parking expansion configurations, and other issues, potentially associated with a future large hospital expansion, and the necessary adjustments for a rezoning. A "Plan B" was forming, and CEO Holly Hill, LLC would fund the re-zoning and new construction so the Landlord can accomplish its desired quick, profitable exit.

After the eviction, Tenant, CEO Holly Hill, LLC, through counsel, brought a legal action against the Landlord, Holly Hill Owner, LLC, for the egregious actions and decisions cited above. The action initially returned to Norwalk Housing Court where the eviction process started in 2016 under the retired Judge Rodriguez. The Landlord (now defendant) sought a summary judgment and dismissal against the Tenant (plaintiff). A successor to Judge Rodriguez had not been appointed.

Swindle. As we were awaiting the successor to Judge Rodriguez in late 2017 and early 2018, I explored the concept of "swindle" as it seemed to encompass these abusive business interactions. The term "swindle" means to cheat a person out of property or defraud or obtain money by fraudulent acts or activities. Swindling is a crime committed by a swindler ("grifter") who defrauds another causing financial damage by means of bad faith, non-disclosure, false pretense, or the use unscrupulous trickery to cheat and defraud.

From this perspective, CEO Holly Hill, LLC was swindled out of its long-term business by the fraudulent, secretive, and deceptive tactics of the Landlord and its Managing Member: no disclosure, no honesty, just bad faith. Tenant became a captive revenue source that would allow Landlord to shift its focus from the class A office sector to medical/hospital in conflict with the existing lease contract.

Captive Tenant would also provide the funding for Landlord to wait for Stamford Hospital to develop its plans and requirements for the 33,000 square feet of vacant second floor space in the building. At that point, the building could be reintroduced to investor candidates already identified in the late 2014 offering.

After focusing for a time on this assessment, I sent the "swindled" conclusion to the Greenwich Police Department, which referred me to the State's Attorney in Stamford, Richard Colangelo, on December 21 for his review and comments. We talked at length on Monday morning, January 8, 2018.

He had read all the information I had sent regarding Landlord's behaviors and my assertion of "swindle", a "criminal" activity. Somewhat apologetically, Attorney Colangelo responded: "This is actually a 'civil' matter involving a contract and breaches of a contract. I am sorry to report this given the number of lease defaults, and breaches you experienced. This number of defaults, breaches and departures from the office lease contract should have supported a strong case in civil court."

Given this rather unexpected assertion from the State's Attorney, it became obvious again the "Merger Clause" in the lease was immediately played to great success by the Landlord and its two law firms. Any verbal promises or marketing statements not written in the lease are not accepted by the court. However, it was a detailed office lease. The extensive record of lease defaults was delivered to the court in testimony and documents. Town rezoning stated: "Landlord has given up on the office market." The record of these facts should have been considered in some detail. They were not.

On a personal level, I had difficulty explaining to family members and the CEO Holly Hill partner what occurred over the 2016-2017 period. Everyone had visited the CEO Holly Hill suite and witnessed events and seminars. They also knew of the arbitration and the police assault, and frequently asked, "How does this happen?"

To assure full disclosure and get questions answered, I arranged for an early January 2018 meeting with Attorney Medico to have an informal discussion with me, my wife, and my daughter, who would come up from Princeton, NJ where we were planning to move in a few months. The meeting took place in his new office in Greenwich Office Park, in a suite once known as Corporate Executive Offices. Tony greeted us as we arrived and took us to a conference room where many documents were arranged on a large table.

After introductions, he advised, "I have answers here, right on the table, to any possible questions you might have, thanks to Frank and my staff. We have nothing to hide. But let me be quite direct. Frank has gotten 'screwed': blatant dishonesty, manipulation, fraud. The list goes on, much of it totally illegal. It's all right here in the documents already submitted to the Court and will be resubmitted to assert the PJR claim for financial restitution."

LESSON

Landlord Had Violated Connecticut Unfair Trade Practices Act

In 1973, the State of Connecticut instituted the Connecticut Unfair Trade Practices Act ("CUTPA"). The law, detailed in Connecticut General Statutes, section 42-110b, provides that "no person shall engage in unfair methods of competition and unfair or deceptive acts or practices in the conduct of any trade or business." A cause of action for a violation of CUTPA comes about when "an ascertainable loss of money or property, real or personal, as a result of the use or employment of methods, acts or practices prohibited by CUTPA."

CUTPA provides for punitive damage awards as stated in the General Statutes: "the court may, in its discretion, award punitive damages as it deems necessary and proper. The evidence must reveal a reckless indifference to the rights of others or intentional and wanton violation of those rights. CUTPA statutes do not provide a method for determining punitive damages. As a result, courts award punitive damages in amounts equal to actual damages or multiples thereof."

Attorney Medico also expressed his apprehensions about the post-recession Connecticut Court system, as he had before the eviction. Judicial staff reductions and justices seeking to retire raised concerns.

Rumors of a Norwalk Housing Court closure had occurred. With Judge Rodriguez retired and no known replacement, Norwalk Housing Court became far less appropriate for the case.

Medico sought to move the case to the Stamford Superior Court, a larger, well-staffed and more sophisticated venue to assess and confront these numerous, far-reaching commercial contract defaults and violations of law. He was convinced the legal violations went well beyond the numerous documented contract breaches. Issues of non-disclosure, deception and fraud brought the confrontation into the realm of the Connecticut Unfair Trade Practices Act, which defines these behaviors as unlawful and subject to punitive damages. A Stamford Superior Court venue with a broader perspective was more appropriate.

Judge Douglas Mintz of Superior Court, on his own accord, held a conference and hearing on the issue of proper venue. On the record, Counsel strongly opposed the Housing Court venue for these complicated assertions of lease violations, contract breaches, unfair trade practices violations, bad faith, unjust enrichment, and the unaddressed pre-judgment remedy.

Douglas Mintz had been a prominent resident of Norwalk for many years. He began his legal career in Norwalk. He was Chairman of the town's Conservation Commission and later an elected member of the Connecticut House of Representatives from Norwalk, before his appointment as a Judge in Superior Court. He had many well-established relationships in Norwalk. It was not clear if he was a completely neutral arbiter of these circumstances.

Landlord's Counsel, DePanfilis & Vallerie, a firm headquartered in the building adjoining the Norwalk Court with partners in frequent contact with the judges and the clerical staff, took the opposite position. It was a lease contract. The Merger Clause in the lease was the overriding provision in this conflict.

Judge Mintz, in his opinion, stated that the lease was the foundation of the case, so Norwalk Superior Court, Housing Session, was the requisite venue.

On September 6, 2018 Counsel, on behalf of CEO Holly Hill, LLC, submitted to the Norwalk Housing Court, Docket No. NWH-CV-17-6002274-S, a detailed response in opposition to Holly Hill Owner, LLC's motion for summary judgment, and dismissal of the pre-judgment remedy.

Material issues of fact required a denial of Landlord's motion for dismissal. Holly Hill Owner's principal defrauded, deceived, and manipulated CEO Holly Hill, LLC, and its principal. Such deceptive conduct was unethical and unlawful within the meaning of the Connecticut Unfair Trade Practices Act (CUTPA). These numerous well-documented violations should allow the court to proceed to a trial wherein CEO Holly Hill, LLC can prove damages, most importantly, the loss of its business (Corporate Executive Offices), the value of improvements and physical assets, marketing initiatives, and other investments made prior to the Landlord's unlawful behaviors and breaches of contract.

The Landlord's fraudulent and deceptive conduct disrupted a valid contract and led to unjust enrichment, as again presented to the Court:

- The opposition to Holly Hill Owner, LLC, Defendant, on behalf of CEO Holly Hill, LLC, Plaintiff, contains well-documented facts, an extensive presentation of case law and precedents, as well as affidavits from the Managing Member, Plaintiff's broker, and veteran experts in the co-working and flex-space field. The legal submission totaled 69 pages and the lease contract. It further referenced scores of prior communications, public announcements, marketing materials, atrium seminar events and other supporting documents previously submitted to the Court. Confirmation of the building's sale in July 2017 was included.
- The Landlord abandoned its contractual commitment to an office building without any notice (Page 7, Article 3) and thereby defaulted after the building did not sell when offered for sale in late 2014. The marketing of the building's class A office

space ceased early in 2015 without any notice, and all office space marketing panels were removed from the atrium lobby in mid-2015. Stamford Hospital began moving its furniture and equipment into its new offices on Level C in late 2015 without any prior announcement.

- Landlord defaulted on its contractual lease commitment to the office building when it ceased all necessary "first class office building Greenwich CT" repairs in 2015 (page 10, Article 5) and abandoned all defined, Building Standard cleaning specifications for the "first class office building Greenwich CT" (Exhibit A).
- Landlord defaulted on the contractual lease commitment to office tenants when it ignored the explicit requirements regarding Building Changes (Page 25, Article 14.4) and Building Standards (Exhibit A, Article 1). All capital improvements to bring the 1980s corporate headquarters building to current class A office standards ceased in early 2015: a.) no garage drainage refinements for flood prevention, no new ceiling panels, no elevation of garage fire sprinkler system to conform to current vehicle height standards, no upgrade of security systems at garage entrances; b.) no repair or cleaning of atrium skylights long covered with mold and dirt, and c.) no modernization and expansion of public restroom installations to 21st century standards of plumbing, toilet flush controls, hand sanitization, cleanliness, and greater daily utilization by occupants and visitors.
- Multiple dated photographs and video footage support these assertions: flooded garages, collapsed garage ceiling panels, overflowing toilets, broken towel dispensers, and an absence of functional soap dispensers and sanitation in the public restrooms. Many Tenant and client complaints had been directed to Landlord and property management on these and related matters.
- Finally, the Landlord (and its successor) would continue defaulting on numerous other contractual obligations in the remaining term of the CEO lease: the Covenant of Quiet Enjoyment, Hazardous Materials (page 11, Article 6), Rules and Regulations (page 14, Article 8), Parking (page 39, Article 31.4), Building Rules and Regulations for Common Areas (Schedule 2), etc. The building had been sold in July 2017 and was now owned by an operator of medical and hospital properties.

On October 1, 2018, less than a month after Attorney Medico's submission to the Court, and 15 months after the sale, Judge Walter Spader, Jr., the recently appointed successor to Judge Rodriguez, issued an Order dismissing CEO Holly Hill's claims without any hearing, to the benefit of Holly Hill Owner, LLC.

Judge Spader's brief statement focused on the "second floor" rezoning and drew heavily from Judge Rodriguez's conclusions from the lease's Merger Clause (Section 37.1) whereby all agreements and understandings between the parties must be written in the lease in accordance with CT General Statutes Section 52-550. It was evident Judge Spader had not reviewed any of Attorney Medico's submissions on behalf of CEO Holly Hill, LLC, the Plaintiff, and the implications under CUTPA.

As a result of Judge Spader's conclusions, the Landlord could do anything it desired as long as it is not explicitly prohibited in writing in the lease, as follows:

- The Landlord (and its successor) can (and will) quietly give up and depart the office market without notice or consideration of the existing office tenants under lease in the building, including the first and largest office tenant with a significant financial exposure.
- The Landlord can ignore the carefully crafted provisions of the office lease contracts.
- The Landlord can default on property management, maintenance and repairs, cleanliness of necessary public areas, and the needed capital improvements to be current and functional.
- The Landlord can ignore the contractual Covenant of Quiet Enjoyment of the office space.
- The Landlord can secretly conspire to rezone and redevelop the building for a use completely incompatible with the commercial office environment detailed in the contracts with tenants.

CUTPA went Kaput. These were the conclusions of Norwalk Superior Court. The financial consequences to Tenant of the Landlord's unlawful actions were ignored.

While the rezoning effort focused on the second floor, the Landlord's abandonment of the office market in late 2014, and the assertive and secretive rezoning effort created a financial trap from which I could not extricate myself or my business. The Norwalk Superior Court format was unresponsive to facts, documents, testimony, and memoranda of law delivered over 18 months.

Perpetrator of this financial entrapment and fraud was ClearRock Properties. The sole mission with the investment was a low budget "quick flip." Recent "quick flip" successes were promoted in their marketing. It was responsible for the early and extensive "class A" office marketing endeavors, the solicitation of Corporate Executive Offices to the Atrium suite, and the non-disclosure of Stamford Hospital's early presence on level C (two months prior to the CEO lease signing).

It managed the early and secretive planning for the rezoning petition and related engineering studies and neglected numerous defaults on the contractual commitments of the office lease especially, maintenance, repairs, necessary capital improvements, and other obligations for to a quality office environment. We soon concluded that the Landlord's team really did not know much about real estate investment management and operations.

It was an asset trader. The "quick flip" offering in late 2014 got its desired response. After the "quick flip" lull, the Landlord abandoned all commercial office lease obligations and commitments, and secretly moved in a contrary direction. As a result, CEO Holly Hill, LLC was paying rent and losing its Letter-of-Credit to fund the Landlord's medical rezoning initiative.

It was likely that Benedict Realty Group was lined up for the acquisition in 2015, as the Landlord was working through the rezoning process with Redniss & Mead, Stamford Hospital, and Greenwich zoning counsel. At that time, Tenant's lease was barely two years into its 11-year term. The asset play agenda was approaching its goal with a huge profit looming ahead. The CEO clients would be departing as the 28-year business would close at a loss totaling more than $3 million including legal fees and uncollected receivables.

LESSON

Boilerplate - Merger Clause: Fraud and Consequences

Merger Clause. A review of extensive on-line legal commentary revealed that the Merger Clause (a/k/a The Integration Clause) is a sensitive, problematic, and potentially damaging provision in a contract. Merger Clauses frequently produce "unintended consequences" and, more specifically, "fraudulent inducement."

Legal reports from 2008 through 2014 warn that the Merger Clause must be taken very seriously, and addressed with deliberate, careful attention and focused refinement for the specific circumstances of the contract. The common "boilerplate" Merger Clause can lead to serious "unintended consequences."

In 2008, an attorney wrote "The Integration Clause That Fails: Unintended Consequences." The following is an excerpt:

" The purpose of the Integration Clause is to void any earlier agreements, discussions, negotiations and proposals, and to make the agreement now being entered into and signed by the parties the only agreement between them, or so the parties have thought.

"On its face, the clause bars alteration or modification of the agreement other than by a signed amendment, or so the parties may have thought. However, courts have ruled that such Integration Clauses are not the obstacle to unintended consequences that the parties expect in such agreements."

In 2014, another legal commentator wrote: "The Merger Clause of a Contract."

"To prevent confusion as to what is in a contract and what is not, contracts will contain boilerplate language called 'merger clause' or 'integration clause' which states that the contract itself is the final word on what the parties have agreed to. 'It is the parties entire agreement on this matter, superseding all previous negotiations or agreements.'

"However, there is one important consideration when it comes to merger clauses, the concept of 'fraudulent inducement'. A signatory to an agreement can claim that the reason it signed the contract was the other party's commitments in the contract that defines and supports the underlying endeavor. If the signatory determines that the other party had no intension of fulfilling its commitments, the signatory can claim a 'fraudulent inducement' into signing the agreement. As a result, the particular wording of the merger clause can become the defining element. A very 'general' boilerplate merger clause will not be as protective as a more 'specific' clause drawing attention to particular subjects of concern."

This routine "boilerplate" was clearly a problematic element, already well exposed in legal commentary. Yet it never surfaced in any of the reviews of the leases supporting the business in Greenwich. The leases were well defined by the numerous provisions detailing the class A office management obligations and procedures. The need for supplemental entries never surfaced from counsel.

At 75 Holly Hill Lane, the lease contained 15 provisions committing the Landlord to high quality commercial office space, with a clean and secure environment of "Quiet Enjoyment." We later learned that Stamford Hospital had very privately absorbed the small medical tenant, well before the CEO lease was executed. The fraudulent inducement may have occurred as its lease was being signed.

The legal commentators also report that asserting claims to circumvent the Merger Clause in court can be especially difficult as lower courts will regard the Merger Clause as the overriding provision, or the default clause, in a contract. As a result, assertions of fraud, contract breaches, bad faith, etc. will typically require appeals from the lower court decisions, or movement of the case to a higher court jurisdiction to enable the full presentation of evidence to counter the "boilerplate Merger Clause", and the quick lower court adjudication as a result.

To avoid this conclusion, Attorney Medico aggressively pursued and documented a wide array of commercial and contract breaches obvious to CEO clients, brokers, and other professionals aware of Tenant's situation. He delivered to Judge Rodriguez in Norwalk Housing Court an extensive submittal on behalf of Tenant detailing contract breaches, fraud, non-disclosure and numerous other CUTPA violations. Counsel then pushed for a transfer from Norwalk Housing to Stamford Superior Court, without success.

Finally, in early September, Attorney Medico then delivered a full 69-page submission to Judge Spader, the successor to Judge Rodriguez, which covered all the prior elements, plus affidavits, expert testimonies, case studies, and the record of the building's sale in July 2017.

Yet on October 1, 2018, Judge Spader, without any conference or hearings, issued his decision affirming Judge Rodriguez's earlier conclusions and dismissing our case. The Merger Clause prevailed without any review!

It was clear to Attorney Medico and me that this seemingly innocuous clause 31.7 on Page 38 in the lease was played to success. The undetected, "boilerplate", Merger Clause became a legalized "escape-hatch" provision that caused irreparable damage when it was exposed in the 2016-17 period. As widely reported, the overlooked clause can lead to serious unintended consequences.

Moreover, all submissions by Tenant's counsel supporting a prejudgment remedy were considered irrelevant. Judge Rodriguez and subsequently Judge Spader, on behalf of Superior Court, were clearly not motivated or equipped to process a more arduous and time-consuming presentation of facts, legal evidence, and resulting financial consequences. The "Merger Clause" provided a quick, accepted response and dismissal. If we have a problem, we must appeal to the next level.

The Connecticut Unfair Trade Practices Act (CUTPA) provides that no entity shall engage in unfair methods of competition and unfair or deceptive acts or practices in the conduct of any trade or commerce. A cause of action for a violation of CUPTA accrues when one suffers an ascertainable loss of money or property as a result of the use or employment of deceptive acts or practices.

The CUTPA violations were evident to clients, brokers, and almost every observant professional in the local business sector, except the Judges in Superior Court. The public record that "Landlord has given up on the office market" was ignored by the Court. Landlord's counsel argued to Judge Rodriguez that the rezoning initiated in late 2015 was "only a second-floor matter," nothing more.

However, when Judge Spader arrived at the Court, the building had been sold to an ownership focused exclusively on medical facilities. Details of the sale were reported in the documents. It was certain 75 Holly Hill Lane would be a Stamford Hospital medical building. It was never, ever just a "second-floor matter."

In early 2018, public information for the building described a "visitor-friendly medical building with new building improvements (lobby, garages and amenities). The entire building meets all requirements for medical. An emergency generator is available."

LESSON

Shock and Anger

In the second quarter of 2018, we had moved to Princeton, NJ to be close to our daughter's family, with their three young children. As we were waiting to hear further from Norwalk Superior Court, lingering financial obligations were being satisfied.

We remained in regular communication with Attorney Medico as we awaited The Court's response. In that period, further Court appearances were anticipated, as we expected fresh testimonies, more depositions, and other technical responses to further reinforce the recent submission to the Court for financial restitution under Connecticut's Unfair Trade Practices Act.

While in New Jersey, Counsel and I pursued various approaches to recover months of uncollected rent from many angry and disappointed clients of CEO Holly Hill, LLC. As soon as the Stamford Hospital construction started in 2016, numerous clients stopped paying as they explored relocation options while working from their offices at CEO. Threats of legal action got no response. By the end of 2017, receivables totaled more than $200,000.

After a year of waiting, I received a short e-mail from Attorney Medico, with a one-page attachment. It was Judge Spader's conclusive statement, which reiterated the earlier judgment of

Judge Rodriguez. And, by the way, any recovery of the receivables would now be the property of the former Landlord.

It was devastating. No review, no hearing, nothing, it was over. The business had closed. I had resigned as Chairman of the Chamber. Fifteen years of engagement with the Greenwich business community had abruptly ended. It was a business loss of more than $3 million, and still some legal fees to pay.

We had sustained a robust recovery and growth through the Recession and advanced the prospects for a sale or recapitalization in 2015 or 2016. The sudden awareness of the long-secret rezoning initiative killed all such discussions. Everyone went quiet: clients, investors, and workspace industry colleagues.

I called him immediately. "Tony, I'm shocked. This one-page statement is an insult. Those guys were incompetent and dishonest from the outset. You were there, in the meetings, you know. The Court is unresponsive to the facts. What do we do now? Can we appeal?"

"Frank, I don't have a real explanation for Judge Spader's quick conclusion. It can be appealed. However, you should know I've been told by their counsel that the profits from the sale in 2017 have been distributed to the investors. Holly Hill Owner, LLC. and Just Clear Holly Hill, LLC. are likely empty shells. An appeals process could be long, difficult, and expensive. I am not able to handle it, but I can introduce you to other appeals specialists I know in Connecticut."

"Tony, I can't really explain to anyone what's happened here. I lost more than $3 million and they made some $14 million at my expense. It has been a shocking series of events, a traumatic nightmare with long-term implications. Let me talk it over with family and the partner, but I think this is over. Thanks."

Family anger was intense: "How could you do this? What were you thinking? No contingency plan, totally reckless." At one point, I left the house and walked to church to get away. The disappointment remained, as did the anger. "We don't want to talk about this ever again. Nice guys finish last."

I continue to be challenged to fully explain the events of the decade if I ever have the opportunity. I can only resurrect the words of an ancient diarist: "......... *need three qualifications to be successful: 1.to be able to lie and not get caught, 2. to pretend to be honest, and 3. to breach contracts without pain or guilt. If you do not get caught, it must be good.*"

In retrospect, I think my family feels I exhibited a certain naiveté regarding trust, honesty, good faith, and other elements of personal and business integrity. I had taken too much for granted as I endeavored to respond to the Recession's aftermath. Yet, in truth, it was a decade of deception, dishonesty, incompetence, manipulation, and numerous practices in violation of a Connecticut law; all without any consequences to the unscrupulous participants.

9. LESSONS - EPILOGUE

The Integrity Bubble

As the century's second decade began, we had already endured the "dot.com bubble", the ensuing series of bankruptcies, and the extraordinary scandals of Enron, WorldCom, and Adelphia Communications. The stock market had declined, and investor confidence weakened in the aftermath of these unusual events early in the decade. New regulations were introduced to enhance investor protections.

Soon a new bubble emerged driven again by "irrational exuberance" in response to low interest rates, relaxed lending standards and a seeming financial-sector push to boost the economy. However, home prices peaked in early 2006. The subsequent drop in values prompted increasing foreclosures across the country. The reverberating financial consequences of the bursting "housing bubble" rippled through collateralized debt obligations, mortgage lenders, commercial banks, hedge funds and Wall Street titans.

Suddenly, Bear Stearns, Lehman Brothers, AIG, Washington Mutual and others succumbed in late 2008. A financial collapse had occurred, largely driven by greed, misinformation, and dishonest manipulation. Then, in December 2008, we learned of Bernard Madoff and his massively fraudulent 20-year ponzi scheme, spotted in 2003 but finally exposed as his investors sought to quickly retrieve their holdings in the financial turmoil.

Legislation was soon introduced to address the widely reckless behaviors of the period and restore some level of trust and honesty in the markets. The Fraud Enforcement and Recovery Act was signed by President Obama in May 2009. In July 2010, the Dodd-Frank Wall Street Reform and Consumer Protection Act was enacted to "promote the financial stability of the United States." Many states, such as Connecticut, had statutes in place to protect against and respond to unfair trade practices.

In Greenwich's long insulated zone of wealth, everything sank to new lows the aftermath of the Lehman bankruptcy. Incomes, public tax revenues, occupancy rates, employment levels, and property values fell sharply. Behavioral patterns, in this unexpected environment, became erratic and combative. Relationships frayed in the newly contentious and adversarial atmosphere.

These area-wide tensions escalated as the recession intensified and continued well into the aftermath. Local businesses shrunk or vanished. Financial sector tenants departed. Parking lots went vacant. Bankruptcies soared. Revenues and cash flow declined everywhere. Buildings remained open, but renovation and revitalization efforts were suspended, and staffing was reduced. Tenant businesses, struggling to survive, were challenged to "pay your rent" as landlords were in denial. Legal counsel seeking resolutions for tenants were often rebuffed by landlords' counsel focused on legal processes for quick review and closure.

The State, long recognized for its favorable tax rates and financial inducements for big-business enterprises, encountered a steep tax revenue decline in the recession and its aftermath. The new realities necessitated cost reductions impacting all public, administrative, and judicial services. The State's civil justice system struggled to maintain judicial responsiveness while burdened by large budget cuts, retiring judges, fewer support staff and increased demand. Small businesses, with limited financial resources, were challenged to confront the well-capitalized big businesses in this conflicted judicial context.

In this period, Corporate Executive Offices had already become a well-regarded and profitable local office-services endeavor, first known as an "executive office suite" business center. The business prospered in the prominent suburban area known for its executives, financiers, traders and affluent "baby-boomers".

The popular, well-capitalized business functioned in prime commercial office buildings under long-term leases secured by large letters-of-credit. The lease contracts obligated the landlords to specific operational standards to assure the tenant of a high quality, carefully managed office environment with an atmosphere of "Quiet Enjoyment" for the lease term. Non-Disclosure Agreements were introduced to reinforce confidential handling of private financial and business information by all parties.

Yet, the Tenant's operations were vulnerable to the decisions, competence, and investment goals of the landlord, often with little regard for lease provisions and the contractual requirements for maintaining the office building environment. Landlords often failed to review contracts or undertake routine property inspections and market analyses prior to multi-million-dollar acquisitions.

Actual market conditions, contractual obligations, and capital needs for the property were often overlooked or not addressed in a timely manner. Tenant would confront erroneous or incomplete invoicing, deferred maintenance, neglected code requirements, and an uninformed sense of the real local economy. These issues produced unexpected confrontations between the Tenant and its landlords.

The sudden financial collapse triggered a series of bizarre and costly encounters with the distractions and risks of a personally managed local enterprise, even as the business itself was successfully responding to new service needs and client expectations in the post-crisis period. As events evolved, unprofessional, manipulative, or dishonest behaviors emerged in many varied situations. Responses could be thwarted by small, overlooked provisions in agreements.

The story is the fifteen-year history of Corporate Executive Offices (CEO), an early entry in the "executive office suite" business model of the 1990s. From 2003 onward it evolved into an admired and valued local force in the expanding serviced office space and co-working world. In response to new technologies, demographic shifts, and new business formats, it transformed into a refined shared offices, collaboration, flex-space, and seminar venue. Customized technology enhancements helped capture many new aspects of office demand to serve a much more diverse clientele.

Throughout the recession's chaotic aftermath, the business rebounded and grew, paid its rent, and supported the class A office goals of the landlords. CEO became the community's "meetings location" for the Chamber of Commerce, the Board of Realtors, seminar organizers, and many others. This contemporary business model is now a global phenomenon with a presence in markets around the world.

Nevertheless, the endeavor offered a badly timed introduction to the contentious, and troublingly complex world of interactions with landlords, partners, lawyers, and the civil court system in the post-recession tensions. Landlords typically have large, patient financial resources ready for a conflict. Partners may be investors and friends but can quickly become protesters and adversaries when advancing personal agendas with vexatious claims.

Moreover, the business' core foundations, long-term lease contracts, were repeatedly undermined and finally destroyed by landlords' inexperience, contract breaches, dishonesty, and fraud. And everyone involved in the property market sought quick financial recoveries: new commissions, new fees, and quick profitable sales; all without new costs, or full disclosure.

It is also the story of a terrific business devalued and brought to closure by malicious claims and devious behaviors on the part of partners and landlords whose lawyers asserted small, overlooked clauses in contracts to justify such behaviors. In the final encounter, the lower court system was quickly dismissive, forcing a troubling decision on the lengthy, expensive appeals processes needed to potentially accomplish an equitable resolution.

At the time, few in this region recognized the enormous potential of the business center, flex-workspace, and co-working industry with new demographics, internet technology, and the emerging "Sharing Economy." Many landlords in the area were especially slow to respond.

A popular, profitable, and very contemporary business with scores of loyal clients became a victim of blatantly dishonest financial manipulations late in the period. Issues of trust, honesty and justice became paramount as Tenant-CEO was bound to a long-term lease with a large financial exposure, and no practical exit.

As we were managing these anxieties on a direct, personal level, we learned about admired athletes' use of performance enhancing drugs to illegally elevate careers and Olympics performance. The global awareness of illegal doping in sports was exposed in numerous public reports and documentaries.

Soon opioid abuse became a widely reported national crisis leading to numerous consequential legal actions against big pharmaceutical companies involved in production and distribution. The slowly evolving disclosure that a prestigious American consulting firm was retained over a long period to advise on opioid development and marketing, added to the epidemic's "crisis of accountability".

The Theranos health care scandal surfaced in 2014: a "massive fraud" involving invalid technologies for blood testing after raising hundreds of millions from investors. In 2016, the Wells Fargo account fraud scandal emerged involving the creation of millions of fraudulent savings and checking accounts. A prominent Wall Street firm's bribery scandal introduced the Foreign Corrupt Practices Act, likely an international version of domestic Unfair Trade Practices Acts.

We learned of the college enrollment cheating scandal involving numerous affluent families. Major League Baseball's 2017 season and World Series were tarnished by "sign stealing" with repercussions on management and players. Scam episodes, of various types, were now reported with surprising frequency.

The consequential financial disclosures of the WeWork enterprise bought considerable press attention to the global workspace industry. The commentary on the founding entrepreneur and his financial sources left some landlords uncertain of the shared workspace format and its management challenges, even as numerous more traditional versions were successfully expanding though the new economic environment.

In the meantime, the "Arbitration Clause" became a controversial and often abused provision in commercial agreements and employment contracts. The arbitration process can be manipulated, knowing that the issue cannot be brought into a court jurisdiction. The confidentiality requirements of the American Arbitration Association are often ignored.

In another context, we learned that the "Merger Clause" in a contract frequently produces "unintended consequences" and, more specifically, "fraudulent inducement." Both clauses were introduced by state judicial systems to expedite dispute resolutions and minimize conflicts but often produced just the opposite.

These boilerplate provisions buried deep in the standard agreements, and not flagged by counsel, brought matters into an unnecessary and lengthy arbitration, and later a consequential legal encounter, both at enormous business and personal cost. Such boilerplate can prevail over all contractual commitments, underlying economic values, and even Connecticut's Unfair Trade Practices Act.

We later revisited the concept of "swindle", a crime committed by a person who defrauds another causing personal or financial damages by means of bad faith, abuse of trust, false pretense, or fraudulent acts. To swindle is to cheat or steal. Yet, to assert a swindle crime, the swindled party must confront the "grifter" in the civil court system, where an existing Merger Clause can likely prevail.

When the business center venture was first acquired, an array of risks was identified and tested: market trends, occupancy history, competition, rent levels, income growth and capital needs. Each risk element was subsequently addressed at regular intervals with partners and bankers in an era of unpredictable and often disruptive change. Various industry sources often added helpful insights.

At the beginning, issues of landlord's management competence, non-disclosure, contract defaults, fraud, or unfair trade practices never surfaced in these many discussions. The focus was the economy, its abrupt change, the recovery, occupancy, rental rates, and future growth that created the early risk anxieties.

However, ceilings collapsed at Two Sound View Drive as a result of long-neglected maintenance and obsolescence issues, already well-reported to the landlord. The damages disrupted dozens of client businesses, technical equipment, and private records, necessitating Tenant's quick departure from the property.

At a second location, non-disclosure agreements required by the landlord were ignored by its management team and leasing brokers leading to contract breaches, tortuous interference, and collusion to force the forfeiture of that lease. All were violations of the State's Unfair Trade Practices Act, CUTPA.

At a prominent third location, the ownership eagerly facilitated the installation of office signage and display panels, authorized joint press releases, and provided photographic elements for the Tenant's business website. Tenant's investment in a dedicated emergency generator on an exterior parcel was facilitated by the ownership to assure continuous electrical service during sudden power outages.

Throughout that period, the landlord knew a regional hospital had very privately absorbed a small medical service on a lower floor and was planning for a major expansion in the building in direct conflict with numerous provisions of Tenant's class A office lease contract.

As we celebrated the 25th year as a business center, the business hosted many conferences and seminars in the atrium lobby to re-introduce the unique property to hundreds of regional executives. In the post-recession period of financial adjustments, the CEO business performed well. It paid its rent, responded to the new economy, and embraced the rapid evolution of new workspace formats.

The landlord failed to attend any of these gatherings to further introduce the building. It was secretly pushing a medical rezoning initiative with its engineering and site planning team. The hospital's plans were known to the landlord and its team, and a prospective purchaser had been identified. Without any disclosure or consideration, the building would become a major regional hospital facility, in direct conflict with the class A office lease with eight years remaining on the term.

The business under the lease lost any economic value. Potential investors known to be interested in the business went quiet. And the landlord needed rent and the $967,000 security deposit to fund the capital needed for a parking expansion and the building modifications required under the medical rezoning stipulations.

At the beginning, the distinction between generalist and specialist seemed clear. The generalist is one whose knowledge, aptitudes and skills are applied to a field. A specialist is a person who focuses on one discipline or one branch of a discipline. The medical profession clearly demonstrates the distinction. The primary care doctor is a generalist, typically in family practice. If the medical problem is eyesight, heart issues or a bacterial infection, for example, the doctor immediately directs the patient to the requisite specialist.

In many aspects of the investment world, the distinctions between a generalist and a specialist are difficult to determine. Investors are often generalists, relying on specialists for insights, risk assessments and management. Some trust their own instincts and financial resources. Lawyers are typically generalists, often with a primary focus. The specialist lawyer concentrates on one major discipline.

Unlike the medical profession, a weak economy and related "opportunistic" circumstances often invite generalist investors, lawyers, their advisors, and others to venture into related disciplines without the relevant, hands-on experience in that specialty. Inevitably avoidable missteps and bad decisions occur, often with serious repercussions on others.

As a result, veteran participants in the local business environment may witness mistakes and actions rarely observed before. The distinction between generalist and specialist can soon blur and undermine the appropriateness and reliability of responses to key business and contractual issues. At times, it becomes hard to distinguish between dishonesty and incompetence. Yet, the distinction between the veteran professional and a rank amateur can become unmistakable.

In many aspects of society, prominent personalities seek influential roles for which they have few qualifications. Notoriety and apparent confidence are no substitutes for professionalism and a proven record of serious accomplishments. When the seemingly "gifted" individual emerges as a blatant "grifter", the consequences can be damaging and far reaching.

The highly fluid "sharing economy" will continue to evolve with new demographics, technological elements, workstyle/lifestyle forces, and corporate adjustments to continue the transformation of workspace. Building owners and their commercial occupants, committed to the expanding co-working and flex-space dynamics, must create new "sharing" tenant/landlord agreements. The traditional lease will be put aside as joint venture agreements or co-management arrangements are crafted to assure collaboration and the sharing of mutual goals, risks, and rewards. The investors, lawyers, management, and advisors must carefully review these agreements for any "boilerplate" provisions that could jeopardize the intent or legitimacy of the relationships.

In the "sharing" world, disinformation and defamation are infectious viruses that can inflame business interactions with few proven antidotes. The viruses transmit through personal contacts, and through commentary enabled by the internet and social media, the increasingly robust sharing zones. The arbitration created a ready source of defamation as clients, investors and a landlord were alerted to the former partners' bogus claims, in blatant violation of the confidentiality agreement. Reputation and credibility are always at risk

As the decade ended, dishonesty overtook disinformation in many business meetings and public statements. The very ideas of truth and honesty became fragile elements of many business interactions. Devious and well-capitalized participants seem to get the benefits, not the most honest. Recent polls suggest that most Americans agree that lying has become all too prevalent in society. Signage began to surface in some suburbs, "Truth Not Lies" and "Honesty Always." Risk/reward analyses are challenged by this new reality.

A rogue traffic control officer's assault put me in the hospital for two days with painful injuries. The traumatic event produced more defamatory assertions in the local media, along with a bizarre infection episode and finally heart surgery. The quick media report and the written police record were total fabrications that bore no resemblance to the actual event, which had been captured on a video provided to legal counsel and the court.

The decade witnessed the closure of a 30-year business, swindled out of existence by a manipulative and unscrupulous landlord. Revisionist history became synonymous with "fake news" at times. Dishonest assertions were frequent and repeated in several different contexts. Well documented evidence of fraud, contract breaches, and other CUTPA violations could not be addressed in Superior Court. The brief Merger Clause was opened to allow the grifter to quietly depart with a very substantial profit, and no consequences.

This period also witnessed the erosion of two 25-year friendships borne of many shared family experiences in our Connecticut town. A Member's repeated disregard for confidentiality and the weak responses to the realities of the recession left their former friend vulnerable to assertive landlords, and unexpected financial costs. Their resurrection of the boilerplate arbitration clause with numerous false accusations produced a costly, two-year conflict completely dismissed and declared to be malicious, vexatious, and defamatory.

Other rogue behaviors surfaced unexpectedly. A competitor secretly visited and evaluated the CEO business in the early recession environment, assisted by on-site intermediaries. Brokers and agents competed for hard-to-find commissions at every opportunity, without regard to existing Non-Disclosure Agreements. The business' private financial information was routed to a competitor and others.

It is difficult to understand what has happened to the basic values of trust, honesty and fair play in business, sports, or public life. Is lying and cheating the new normal? With financial resources and responsive lawyers, rogue players can push the system, without consequences. A budget-stressed judicial system was unresponsive to flagrant violations of Connecticut's Unfair Trade Practices Act.

Another lingering question continues to resonate. How much do professional relationships, and possibly social interactions, between lawyers and the judges in their courts influence judicial actions and decisions? Legal counsel was well acquainted with the Superior Court judge assigned to address the misdemeanor charges. He was pleased. The favorable response was anticipated.

The legal firm representing the Holly Hill landlord was long-established in Norwalk Superior Court with its offices adjoining the Courthouse. Many cases had been tried by the firm before Judge Rodriguez and others in Norwalk Court. Efforts by Tenant's counsel to move the case to Stamford Superior Court were dismissed by a judge with a history of legal and community involvement in Norwalk.

Who or what can be trusted? It seems hard to know or explain. Much has been written about these unusual behavior patterns. As highlighted in the introduction, Professor Shiller is concerned about "How Lying and Mistrust Could Hurt the American Economy."

Michiko Kakutani also writes in the New York Times: "The 2010s Were the End of Normal - A Decade of Distrust." In it she writes of "portents of disorder; fear and distrust are ascendant." In conclusion she adds, "The biggest casualty of the decade was trust." We have recently learned that psychologists are now focusing on dishonesty to find "The Good, the Bad and the Radically Dishonest."

As we reflect on the past two decades, we endured the "dot.com bubble", and next the "housing bubble." Could America be confronting another bubble, an "integrity bubble?" Integrity incorporates trust, honesty, and respect. Integrity is the practice of being honest and showing consistent and uncompromising adherence to strong moral principles and values in one's actions.

In the workspace of the future, almost everything will be shared: space, technology, services, and relationships. Workplaces will be redesigned for activities benefiting face-to-face interactions including collaboration on projects and training. Common areas will increase in size. Furniture and equipment will be easily relocated as needs change. Traditional desks and file cabinets are gone. Computer screens will dominate on versatile worksta-tions. Small phone booths will allow for private calls. In this evolving new office space format, trust and honesty will be es-sential in a continuously shared environment. An atmosphere of integrity will be a crucial to the success of these workspace enterprises.

Integrity is an asset that has been highly valued by society for generations. It is a foundation of our culture supported by many varied financial and social initiatives, and legal mandates. My family would say I have invested in Integrity with some "irrational exuberance", as have many others. Is the "integrity bubble" bursting? If that is happening, what could be the conse-quences? What can be done now to restore Trust and Honesty, and preserve Integrity and Justice for everyone? It is a deeply troubling concern needing a collective, unified response.